Praise for *THEY'RE F*

"Thank you, Liz for celebrating ... .ggle of saying goodbye. This book is a reminder that heading off to college or university gives us permission to discover new ways to care for and love our children. Read this if you are sending a loved one away to a new educational experience – it is a salve for your relationships away and back at home."
KENNETH ELMORE, Associate Provost and Dean of Students at Boston University

"From learning how to deal with seniors getting ready to leave the nest to understanding a new parental role, Liz Yokubison has done a great job helping parents navigate one of the hardest seasons of raising children. If you have kids, you need this book. If you have high school kids, you need this book. If you have seniors, it's a necessity to have this book."
ANDY BRANER, President KIVU Gap Year; Author *No Fear in Love: Loving Others the Way God Loves Us, Alone: Finding Connection in a Lonely World, Love This, and Duplicate This.*

"The essential guide for parents sending kids to college is here! Pack their bags with love and tools to spare, and gain a deep reservoir of strength, peace and joy for yourself."
HEATHER SIMONSEN, KSL TV Reporter, 2-time Emmy winner, 4 nominations from the National Association of Television Arts and Sciences.

THEY'RE
READY.
ARE YOU?

THEY'RE

READY.

ARE YOU?

*A Parent's Guide to Surviving the
College Transition*

LIZ YOKUBISON

Published in the United States by

Kindle Direct Publishing (KDP)

ISBN-13: 9781731060006
Library of Congress Control Number: 2018913879

Cover design by VSA Partners

Headshot by Dulce Photography

Dedication

To Alex and Morgan, without you this book never
would have been written. To Ron, for always believing
in me and encouraging me to chase my dreams.
The three of you are everything to me.

CONTENTS

Acknowledgements   13

Introduction   17

Chapter 1: Senior Year   21

Choosing a College
The Senior Year Experience
Learn from Me, Grasshopper
A Summer Bucket List
Have Your Student Create a Budget

Chapter 2: College Orientations   44

A Glimpse into Their New Life
Easing Their Anxiety
Make the Most of Your Time on Campus
Dorm Options
Finding a Roommate
What Do They Really Need to Take to College?

Chapter 3: Saying Goodbye   62

Ask Them What They Want
There Will Be Tears
Another Family's Goodbye
Self-Care Once You Are Back Home

Chapter 4: Building a Strong Marriage   78

Why Is Strengthening Your Marriage Important?
Weekly Date Nights
Romantic Weekends Away
Finding Mentors
Cultivating Couple Time with Others

Chapter 5: Staying In Touch   97

How Much is Too Much?
Alternatives to Phone Calls
One Truly Creative Approach

Chapter 6: Siblings Still at Home   108

What It Feels Like
Don't Hide Your Grief
More Advice
It's OK to Be Excited

Chapter 7: Visiting Your College Student   120

The Big Kahuna: Campus Visit #1
Campus Visit #2
Subsequent Visits
If You Can't Visit

Chapter 8: Your New Role   131

What Does Coaching Look Like?
Support When You're Not There
Summer after Freshman Year

Chapter 9: First Visit Home   148

When Your Child Is Ready To Come Home
When Your Child Would Rather Be at School

Chapter 10: First Holiday Apart   159

Create New Traditions as a Couple
Serve Others
Encourage Your Kids to Create New Traditions

Chapter 11: Reinventing Yourself   167

    Surrogate Kids
    Discovering New Interests
    A New Career is Born

Chapter 12: It All Comes Around Again   181

ACKNOWLEDGEMENTS

The genesis for *They're Ready. Are You?* arose from the things I wished I had known when we sent our twins to college. My original purpose was to help other parents going through this major life transition. As I wrote each chapter, another reason came to light. This book became my way of processing the change for myself and our family.

The following people contributed to this book in ways both big and small.

My husband Ron: Thank you for loving me unconditionally, believing in my dream of becoming a published author and making it possible through daily encouragement, guidance and support. I love you.

Alex and Morgan: You not only made me a mom, but also an author. Thank you for letting me share your stories with the world. It is an honor to watch you learn, grow and fully embrace your respective college experiences.

My mom Jan McLaughlin: Thank you for taking me to all the Daughters of the American Revolution (DAR) essay competitions and sitting through endless spelling bees. Those experiences shaped me as a writer and planted the seed to someday write a book.

Ron and Janet Yokubison: Thank you for being loving in-laws who are like a second set of parents to me.

Fellow authors, Heather Simonsen and Abbie Smith: Thank you for encouraging me to self-publish and never look back.

Tiffany Grayson, editor extraordinaire: You made this book better, not only with your thoughtful edits, but by introducing your own observations as a mom sending her eldest to college.

Chrystine Witherspoon and her team at VSA Partners: Thank you for the best book cover any first-time author could dream of and one that only got better when you added EMTY NST to the license plate on the car.

Andy Braner: Thank you for all you've done for our family over the years and for coaching me on everything from the book title to the marketing plan and helping promote this labor of love.

To the moms who graciously shared their personal stories for this book: Cindy, Jeannie, Kristen and Laurel. I am humbled by your honesty and willingness to give me insights into your parenting. I learned so much from each of you.

Last, but not least, thank you to "my girls": Shawna Doughman, Jo Duff, Maribeth Herman, Courtney Hutcheson, Juliy Marie, Lesa Peers and Heather Simonsen. I love you all and cherish your friendships. Thanks for always having my back.

INTRODUCTION

This book is not about how to get your kids into college. Plenty of other resources exist to meet that need. It also isn't designed to get your kids to choose the college that you want them to choose. Instead, this book is to help you prepare yourself, and your kids, for a successful transition from living in their childhood home to living on their own for the first time.

Sending your kids away to college isn't easy. And it isn't supposed to be. After all, you've spent 18, or more, years of your life raising these would-be-adults from teeny tiny babies who depended on you for their every need, to high school seniors who think they don't need you at all.

You've kept them safe through the toddler years — including such gray-hair-inducing situations like preventing them from getting electrocuted when they tried to stick a metal keychain into an electrical outlet. Case in point, the permanent smoke spot on the carpet of one of my kids' rooms. Chances are you've also had more than your fair share of health scares from the croup to raging fevers to the flu. You've probably spent at least one night in the hospital by the bedside of a child with appendicitis, or some other such alarming surgery. And I'm certain you have driven more than a tad bit over the speed limit to get to the ER, stat, because your child suffered a concussion, needed stitches, lacerated a liver or worse.

How do these darling children, for whom you've risked life, limb and financial stability repay you? They abandon you with nary a thought about how much you'll miss them or how quiet the house will be when they are off at college. In fact, they can't get out the door fast enough to start a new chapter in their lives. And that is exactly how it's supposed to be.

This book is intended to help you see what's coming. Starting from the senior year in high school, all the way to their first summer at home, or studying abroad or possibly working in another city. How dare they! Is it the be-all, end-all solution to every challenge you will have as a parent sending your kids into the fun, exciting, exhilarating and slightly scary world of college? Nope. But I sure wish I had a guidebook like this when I was getting ready to let go of my kids in anticipation of the empty nest. In fact, I remember after their first Thanksgiving at home, thinking "why didn't anyone tell me it would be like this?" And that's exactly why I wrote this book.

To be totally transparent, I have twins. When my first went to college, so did my last. Thanks to the grace of God and wonder of modern fertility treatments, my husband and I were blessed with a boy and a girl. My Christian faith helped me tolerate being a human pin cushion, receiving daily shots to become pregnant. It also helped me endure my parents' divorce when I was just 10 years old, and withstand a verbally abusive father. Does that mean you have to share my beliefs to

19

get something out of this book? Not at all. I recognize that religion and spirituality come in many shapes and forms. And I honor that. I mention my faith since it was a big part of my journey through the college transition. Especially with my entire family leaving for college at the exact same time. Ouch!

So while I may not know exactly what it feels like to send your ducklings off one at a time, I can tell you firsthand how different it is with a son and a daughter. How both genders still get their feathers ruffled. And how it feels to become an empty nester.

Did it hurt more to let both my kids fly the nest at the same time than when someone with three kids of different ages sends their first or their last to college? I can't honestly say. But I can tell you whether it's your first, last, both at the same time (or more - mothers of triplets I bow down to you), unless you're prepared, sending your kids to college can rock your world.

CHAPTER ONE

Senior Year – The Year of Letting Go

When my son was a toddler, he looked up at me with his big blue eyes and squishy cheeks and said, "Mom, I'm going to marry you and live with you forever!" I remember tears filling my eyes, part wishing it was true and part afraid that it was. And so it feels when your child begins his/her senior year of high school.

If you're like most parents, you've felt an impending sense of dread since they started ninth grade, when you realized, with a jolt, "in four years they'll be gone!" If we're being honest, there were probably also plenty of other times that realization hit you, when they were late for curfew or had friends over who kept you up until 1 a.m., when it actually seemed like a pretty good thing that they'd be leaving home.

But their senior year in high school is a whole different ballgame. Some parents have the best intentions – college visits all wrapped up and applications completed the summer before the final year of high school actually begins. However, despite the best laid plans, fall of senior year is most often a dizzying array of writing essays, submitting college applications, tracking down transcripts, and securing teacher and high school counselor recommendations. Not to mention a full load of AP classes and extracurricular activities, in addition to scholarship and financial aid applications to complete. It is not a walk in the park, no matter how carefully you've planned.

One thing that can make this year easier on everyone in the family, is finding other adults, usually younger ones in their twenties, who can act as mentors for your kids. One couple who intentionally set about this task, as early as middle school, were Cindy and Darren, parents to Irish twins, who were born just 13 months apart. "We purposely reached out to different people we trusted to influence our girls," says Cindy. Oftentimes, their daughters were the ones to mention specific young adults they had fun with. "They really wanted to hang out with these people and we encouraged it since they were at an age where mom and dad had lost their cool factor," Cindy recalls with a smile. Simply put, there will be ups and downs in your child's senior year and it sure helps for them to have other adults to turn to, whom you trust to be a positive influence during this momentous time in their lives.

Choosing a College

Step One: Stop trying to control everything that needs to happen for your child to get accepted into college. This means letting your student take some ownership of the application process, to the degree that he/she is capable and willing, without compromising their admission. From which schools to apply to, completing applications and tracking down all the bits and pieces for an application to be complete, high school seniors certainly have their work cut out for them.

In our case, my husband and I helped our twins determine which colleges to visit, based on a number of factors that varied significantly by child, and then assisted them in narrowing down the list of schools to which they planned to apply. We knew the timing of the application deadlines, but other than occasionally prodding them to make sure they hit the deadlines, we stepped back and let both of them take responsibility for the process. This worked for our family because of the type of kids they were – driven, committed and organized. Also, if I'm being totally honest, it helped that they were twins. Similar to when they applied for their driver's licenses just a mere two years earlier, our kids were competitive enough with each other to make sure that one of them didn't end up with completed college applications while the other was just starting the process.

Some parents told me that they gave their student the illusion that he/she was completely in control of the process, while the parent was actually the safety net to make sure the student didn't miss important deadlines. Just another example of how the process varies by family, and most importantly the potential student.

Since I was a writer, both of my kids wanted me to edit their college essays before submitting them. Don't be too impressed. This was literally the only time either one asked for my writing expertise during their entire four years of high school.

Can choosing a college be a nail biting, sometimes excruciating process to watch from the sidelines? Absolutely. I remember my son receiving a letter from a great engineering college, one that he wasn't even considering, saying they would waive the application fee and the essay requirement if he applied by a certain date. Unbeknownst to us, after dinner that same night, he declared, "I just applied to my first college!"

My husband and I looked at each other, bewildered that he had chosen to do it all by himself, the speed at which he completed the task, and the fact that this particular college wasn't even on his list to consider. It didn't have a Division 1 swim program, which was his primary requirement in selecting a college. A few weeks later, when he was accepted, he was thrilled to tell his friends, "I'm going to college," even though he had no intention of attending that particular school. Imagine our dismay when, a few weeks later, he was offered a generous scholarship from the same university, but wouldn't even consider it due to the swim program.

Frustrating? You bet. Did we push our son to reach out to the coach or visit the campus? Nope. It was just one of the ways that we showed our kids that it was their decision where they chose to go to college. We wanted them to own the process. This meant allowing them to use their gut instincts and list of things they had compiled in their 18-year-old minds that they wanted in their college experience, and then apply and choose accordingly.

Instead of forcing your child's college choice, if you let the process play out organically, it becomes crystal clear where he/she is supposed to go to school. And chances are they will be happier with their decision, than if a particular school was pushed on them. I liken our experience to God shining a light on our children's respective colleges, making it completely obvious which schools were right for each of them. And I have two very different kids – a son who was looking for college-level swimming, an urban campus, and a good engineering program; and a daughter who wanted a traditional college campus with lots of green space, Greek life, and a robust zoology and dance program (a seemingly odd combination that was surprisingly feasible.)

With these prerequisites in mind, my husband and I decided to divide and conquer when it came to college visits. Having been a recruited swimmer in college, my husband took our son to the schools with swim programs that met his other criteria. I became the zoology/marine biology expert and accompanied our daughter on her college tours. With such a specialized major, I thought it might be useful to set up meetings with advisors or professors in the marine bio or zoology departments. This proved to be a huge blessing. After learning about course loads and research requirements, our daughter, who had previously been focused on becoming a marine mammal rescue and rehab scientist, decided that zoology was a better option for her.

After visiting eight schools (in six different states), our daughter started filling out applications. Since her top schools had rolling admissions, she got accepted into the first one she applied to within days. She quickly applied to the next one and heard back within a week, at which point she looked at me and said, "Mom, since I got into my top two schools I really don't think I want to apply anywhere else." Could I have insisted she apply to the six schools that she visited that remained on her list? Yes, but why? She knew in her gut these were her two favorites. Plus, she still had to decide between the two she'd been accepted to, which took some time given the different degree programs, widely varied dance programs, and that they were in two very different states, with hugely diverse climates and geography.

Step Two: Once your student starts receiving his/her college acceptance letters, make sure you are there to provide a little guidance, so they don't feel totally alone in choosing which college to attend. After our daughter received her acceptances, she struggled with how to determine which school was right for her. Was the fact that she had cried upon opening the email admitting her to the second college perhaps a sign that was the place for her? We gently suggested that one factor wasn't enough to make a decision on where she would get her bachelor's degree and spend the next four years of her life. Instead, we recommended that she make a pro/con list (just like the ones Rory Gilmore used so famously in *Gilmore Girls*), told her to pray about the decision, and then reminded her of her strong intuition, which had served her well over the years.

Weeks later, our daughter casually mentioned at the dinner table that she still couldn't decide. Even though she had done her pro/con list and prayed about which college was right for her, the decision was weighing on her heavily. When we offered to go over the list with her, she looked at us in all seriousness and said, "But, I thought I had to make the decision all by myself." My husband and I looked at each other, in one of our less-than-stellar parenting moments, as we suddenly realized we had never told our daughter that we could discuss the list together. Instead, the poor girl literally thought she had to decide her entire collegiate future, all by herself without input from us. As I've said ever since I started raising kids, you do the best you can and therapy will take care of the rest. A note to future therapists of my children: I really didn't see most mistakes, like this one, until they were in the rear view mirror of life. Honest!

Even though it is so incredibly competitive to get into college these days, university administrators have figured out how to make prospective students, and their parents, feel as comfortable as possible with their decisions. If your child is struggling with choosing which of the colleges to attend where he/she has been accepted, another great thing to do is to (re)visit the campus, if at all possible. Most colleges have specific times when students are invited for Admitted Student Days, and often have clever names like Choose CSU Days or Duck Days (University of Oregon.)

The entire schedule is designed to help your student decide which institution is right for them. Not only do the kids get lots of swag from the school, but they have an opportunity to interact with current students and learn about various clubs and organizations, specific to their interests. If prospective students have a general idea of their major, they can even attend presentations by that academic department to learn about types of classes required, class sizes, living and learning communities (dorms designated for specific majors), and a myriad of other facts and figures. You even get to eat lunch in one of the dining halls, and the day usually culminates with a campus tour, including a peek into one, or more, of the dorms. It was during one of these days that our daughter made her decision about which college to attend. No second guessing. Not a shadow of a doubt.

The Senior Year Experience

Just like selecting where to go to college, there are a myriad of things during your student's final year at home, where you need to step back, bite your tongue, and see how it all unfolds. This is especially true with exactly how much – or how little – they want to accomplish during their senior year. For some kids, it's "just" about getting into college and spending as much time with their friends – making memories during the final football or basketball seasons, bonfires, Homecoming and Prom dances. For others, it's about how they've visualized their last year in high school: special awards and recognition, how many cords they can accumulate to wear over their cap and gown on graduation day, and maybe attaining a goal they've been striving toward for the last four years. Whether you have one of these types of seniors or a child somewhere in between, this final year of high school can be hard on you as a parent. Your student will most likely spend a lot less time at home hanging out with you and his/her siblings than they have in years past.

Parents of kids who just want to make the most of their senior year often worry about parties, drugs, drinking, and sex. All of these are valid concerns for parents of any high schooler, and these days, sadly, even middle schoolers. But when you're dealing with a high school senior, in the space of less than a year, they will be living away from home in an environment where all the same temptations will still be front and center, even more so. Does this mean you should encourage them to have kids over and provide alcohol and give them the run of the house? Absolutely not. But it does mean you can offer them a fun, safe, drug- and alcohol-free environment where they can (and hopefully will want to!) come hang out with their buddies. And to be honest, this starts in the early years of high school.

Some recommendations based on my experience: Find a teen-friendly space in your home, like a garage, basement, or outside space if you live somewhere warm. Load it up with games and activities that teenagers, including high school seniors, would enjoy. Yes, that means the dreaded X-Box, but also fun activities that allow them to burn off some energy – a ping pong table, foosball table, or pool table can provide hours of entertainment and can often be purchased inexpensively at garage sales. Never underestimate the power of a good old-fashioned basketball hoop or a place to play football or ultimate Frisbee outside, if space allows. Then stock a small fridge or cooler with teenager-approved, non-alcoholic drinks (flavored La Croix was a big favorite at our house), offer them endless amounts of snacks and pizza (as your budget permits), and let them just hang out. This gives you the added advantage of being a fly on the wall, catching snippets of their conversations, or becoming a surrogate parent to their friends who may need a listening ear from a trusted adult. Side note, if opposite sexes are involved, be sure to pop in unannounced at regular intervals, have younger siblings do the same, or send in the family dog, to let them know this is a G-rated environment.

For the potentially over-achieving high school seniors who want to be in four different extracurricular activities at once, participate in service projects, and apply for high school awards, all while completing the requisite 8-10 college applications, parenting can be just as challenging. Before you stop reading, hear me out. While parents of these kids may not worry about the party scene, because quite frankly, this type of student barely has enough time to sleep, let alone socialize, it can be just as hard to try to reign this child in.

As adults it's easy to look at the cacophony of opportunities your child has chosen to pursue and try to convince them to just skip one. You worry about them getting sick, stressed out, or not enjoying their last year of high school. Worse, you worry that if they don't accomplish all of their goals, they will be deflated, disappointed, or discouraged. To be blunt, one of these things is more than likely to happen to the overachieving student. However, it's better for them to stumble and fall a little while they're still at home where you can help pick them up and brush them off. You won't have that luxury next year when they're living on their own.

What about high school seniors who are just the opposite and seem to be lacking in motivation? Many parents feel the need to push these types of kids into multiple activities to ensure they complete their required service hours, demonstrate proficiency in a sport, and keep taking the ACT or SAT until they get the score that the parents deem acceptable for the "right" college. The reality is that this sort of helicopter parenting can really start to backfire once your child hits his/her senior year. It may be successful for the first semester while your student is submitting applications and has not yet been accepted to college. However, once your child is officially in his/her last semester of high school, chances are he/she may feel resentful of all the pressure and pull away even more. This is probably the last thing you want when you literally only have seven more months of them living at home with you.

Learn From Me, Grasshopper

I'm pretty sure this is a mom thing, but once our kids are seniors in high school we tend to feel the proverbial clock ticking, and we realize we still have so much to teach them before they live on their own. What if they forget to clean the lint trap in their dormitory's clothes dryer and the building burns down? How will they eat well if they have to go back to school early for winter training and the dining halls are closed? Don't laugh, these were just a few of the things I was still offering instructions about to each of my kids when we pulled up to their respective campuses to begin unloading all of their belongings.

In my defense, we did have a few hiccups during their junior and senior years of high school, which made me realize that my parenting job, in terms of teaching life skills, was not even close to complete. Interestingly enough, both situations involved postage, and how to mail packages and envelopes properly. I had this sinking feeling of, "Dear Lord, what else have I failed to teach them?" It was exactly what I needed to feel in order to look at the coming year with the eye of a teacher helping her young Jedis master the skills necessary to succeed in the big, scary galaxy of life.

The first aha moment occurred when my son was preparing to send a birthday gift to a friend out of state.

He wrapped the present and then put it in a shipping box I had retrieved for him from my stash of used Amazon boxes. I helped him seal it and he addressed it to his friend. I had to remind him to put the return address on it, specifically in the upper left-hand corner. Then he asked me for a stamp. I reminded him that he was taking the box to the post office to mail it, when he looked at me with annoyance and said, "Yeah, Mom, I know, but I need a stamp to mail it." That's when it hit me: He had never mailed a package before! In fact, the only time he'd ever used the U.S. Postal Service was to mail the mandatory thank you cards that I required him to send every Christmas and birthday.

Trying not to crack a smile, I explained how, once he got to the post office, they would put the required postage on his package. To which he replied, "Yeah, I know, but I still need a stamp." What followed was a detailed explanation of how the post office clerk would weigh the package and then add a sticker, that wasn't a stamp, with the amount of postage it cost to send the gift all the way to Texas. In a world where technology reigns the lives of teenagers, it actually made sense in the end.

Even though I made sure to tell his twin sister the story, not to make fun of her brother, but as a learning moment so that she, too, would know how to mail a package, another postage incident happened right before Christmas during her senior year. While my husband and I were out of town, our daughter thought she would help by addressing the family's annual Christmas cards, which had arrived just before we left for the weekend. Since we are the lazy (I like to think of it as organized) family who prints out address labels, rather than hand-addressing 120 cards, our daughter started stuffing cards into the envelopes, sealing them, and applying the address labels and stamps. She got through about half the cards. When we returned from our weekend away, I was touched at how thoughtful she had been to lighten my load by starting the Christmas card labeling process. Until I discovered that she'd put all of the address labels in the upper left side of the envelope, where the return address labels should have gone.

Suddenly I remembered that, when she wrote her requisite thank you notes, just like her brother after every Christmas and birthday, I had been addressing them for both kids in an effort to save time. For as long as they could write! So they had, for years, only been applying the stamps to the envelopes themselves. After a deep breath and a good chuckle, I was able to order more envelopes and get more stamps from the post office so we could start the process again. Needless to say, our cards arrived right before Christmas that year, but I can assure you that our daughter now knows, without a doubt, how to properly address an envelope.

A Summer Bucket List

After the chaos of graduation ceremonies and celebrations, your whole family will likely breathe a collective sigh of relief. And it is well deserved. But within a relatively short period of time, you, as parents, will realize that only a few months are left with your soon-to-be-college student at home. Don't panic. With some careful planning and realistic expectations, you can enjoy this "senior summer" without suffocating your recent graduate and still make some great memories as a family.

My first mistake was assuming this summer was going to be relaxing. Little did I know that, in between my kids' work, dance, and swim schedules, I'd make countless trips to Target and the Container Store, stocking up on everything they needed to create a home-away-from-home in their dorm room. Then there were the requisite medical appointments – last dentist appointment timed so they could get their teeth cleaned over Christmas break, physicals from their doctor and, believe it or not, their final vaccinations required to be allowed to actually live on a college campus. Hadn't they already had enough vaccinations in the last 18 years?

And here's the hard part. My recommendation is to let your kids make all of these appointments on their own and go to them by themselves. Why? Because they are adults now, or soon to be, and it's just another life lesson you can teach before they're out of your house. Even more valuable than teaching them about postage.

In the midst of this rather hectic summer, take time to sit down with your child and ask him/her to think about some of the things they would like to do before they go away to school. We called it their Summer Bucket List, and it included things like taking each one to their favorite breakfast place "one last time," and which high school friends they wanted to spend time with before the summer came to an end. While our daughter was taking her last dance classes with her favorite instructor and going on endless lunch and coffee dates, our son embarked on two different overnight backpacking trips. One was with his high school buddies, where they hiked to the highest peak in Utah. The other was with his dad, just the two of them, spending the night under the stars to watch the sunrise on their favorite mountain. Great memories were made, and it was a way of symbolically closing the chapter on the high school season of their lives.

Have Your Student Create a Budget

The last step in your year of letting go, which will further help your child be self-sufficient in the real world, is having them create a budget for the first semester of their freshman year of college. This can include tuition, room and board if your student is helping pay for that, and/or maybe some or all of the other expenses that might be incurred while living away from home. Think books, medical and toiletry supplies, entertainment, and the like. While some kids may already have an idea about the categories of said budget, it's easier to create the list together, during which you'll likely hear interesting comments like, "I forgot I'd need a haircut while I was gone for four months," or "What do you mean I have to make a budget for clothes, don't you buy all of my clothes?"

Once the categories are agreed upon, and they will likely differ by sex of child and type of campus, have them come up with estimates for things like eating out, haircuts, clothes, food for their dorm rooms, etc. We gave each of our kids this assignment at the beginning of the summer and they both came up with their respective budgets just a week before they were due to move away from home. Irritating to parents? Yes. But easily put off by high school seniors who really just want to spend as much time as possible with their friends instead of being bothered with something as benign as creating a budget. The reason our kids finally got them done was because we told them we wouldn't fund their new college checking accounts until they gave us a number, in black and white, and broken out by category, that we could all agree on.

CHAPTER TWO

College Orientations – A "Must" for Parents

Back in the days of old, there were no such things as college orientations. Our parents simply decided what we needed for our dorm rooms, moved us in, and headed on their merry way. So if the idea of attending a college orientation with your child seems like something you can skip, don't be fooled. It is required for every admitted student to attend, and parents are encouraged to join as well. Still, I was surprised at the number of parents who did not attend orientation at either of our twins' schools.

Is it an added expense to travel to campus and stay in a hotel for a night while your child stays in the dorms? Absolutely. However with the latest options of Airbnb and VRBO, a single overnight accommodation can be reasonable. And it is worth every penny, not only to support your college freshman, but to educate yourself on what your student will experience – not just during the week of move-in, but for their entire first year of college.

A Glimpse into Their New Life: Why Parents Should Attend

My husband and I attended not one, but two orientations, at very different colleges, within a span of a couple of weeks and were amazed at how different each experience was. While they both had the same general format – students broken into groups led by orientation leaders and parents armed with a folder and a schedule of endless presentations to choose from – each orientation had a different approach to how the students and parents interacted.

At one school we were seated with our daughter during the opening presentation, which included a video so engaging it made me wish I was back in college. Larger than life on a big screen were vivid photos of existing students, giving a glimpse into the culture and spirit of the university, interspersed with emotive music so well done I literally had chills of excitement at the end. Then the leader showed us a map of all 50 states represented by the Class of 2021 (How did that happen? They were just the class of 2017!) after which our daughter was whisked away while we attended parent breakout sessions, only to be reunited with her for lunch, dinner, and then breakfast the next day.

In contrast, my son's college immediately separated the students from the parents at check-in and had the parents seated above the students in the hockey arena while the kids were all on the main floor. Another impressive video, complete with music that brought tears to my eyes, and included images showing the campus during each of the four seasons, along with sports, activities, and the diversity of the student body. This was followed by a series of speeches from faculty members and concluded with the Dean of Student Affairs, an impressive speaker in his own right, telling us that, for the next 29 hours, the Orientation Team was going to be in charge of our child and asked us very nicely not to text, call, email, Snapchat, or have any other sort of communication with our student so he could be completely immersed in the orientation experience. The dean concluded with these words: "We've been doing college orientations since 1937 and haven't lost a student yet."

To be honest, as soon as we were separated from our kids at each orientation, my husband and I started plotting which presentations we could skip in favor of a workout or grabbing a cup of coffee. But the first parent session ended up being so engaging that we attended (almost) all of the rest. Over the span of the next day and a half, we learned about what to expect the first semester while our child was transitioning from home to college life, from a psychological perspective as well as a social perspective. (Wasn't I just reading *What to Expect When You're Expecting*"?) We also were filled in on the specific classes our students would register for, their course load for the first year, tuition costs and meal plans, financial aid, and more.

Surprisingly, one of the best presentations was from the chief of the college's police department, who explained regulations about minors drinking alcohol on federal land (one of our twins attended a land grant college) and amnesty policies that encouraged kids who attended parties with alcohol to call the campus police if things got out of hand, in exchange for full amnesty. It was this institution's way of making students accountable for helping reduce/eliminate alcohol poisoning, sexual harassment, and assault. Being the parent of a daughter, this session did more to put my fears to rest than all of the other presenters combined!

Jeanne, a mother of two boys and a girl, recalls taking her eldest son to orientation, which happened a few days before classes started, and also helped move him into his dorm. "It was really good for me to be there and have a picture of his room," she says. However, when her second child went to college, she elected to skip orientation and move-in since he was attending the same college as his older brother. Jeanne recalls, "I have this vivid memory of taking them both to the airport and standing there watching them go through the security line and getting further and further away from me. All I could think was that I got my oldest all settled in and I was sending my other son off to college without his mom." Needless to say she attended orientation for her daughter, and also moved her into her dorm room a few years later.

Easing Their Anxiety: Why Students Should Attend

As mentioned before, college orientations are required for incoming freshmen. Some are held at various dates throughout the summer, while other universities start their orientations on move-in day. If your student's summer plans are already full, or more likely, you have visions of a last family vacation together, for your child's sake, make summer orientations, if offered, a priority. Then do everything you can to get your student there.

Why? Because this is really the beginning of your child's college experience. It doesn't start on the first day of classes. Instead, it all starts at orientation. First, they get the chance to make friends, which is huge to reaffirm their college choice. In some instances, the friends they make at orientation will become people they will spend a lot of time with their freshman year. In other cases, if they are placed in dorms on the opposite side of campus, they may not see them regularly, but the important thing is they already have a few people's names and numbers to connect with during their first few weeks of college.

Another reason it is vital for your student to attend orientation is because they will be paired with academic advisors who will actually help register them for their first semester of classes. This helps alleviate a lot of the uncertainty about starting college, simply by knowing their course schedule. Most advisors use the Goldilocks approach for freshmen – they make sure the course load is not too much, or too little, but just right. Best of all, having an advisor literally walk them through the registration process makes it so much easier for your student to register all by him or herself the following term.

Lastly, given the amount of time students traverse the campus during orientation, your child becomes even more comfortable with where everything is and this helps them visualize living there. Dorm tours are usually included in summer orientations so your kids, and you, can really see how small the space is, and hopefully eliminate the potential for bringing absolutely everything from their room at home to college.

Make the Most of Your Time on Campus

If you choose to attend orientation with your student, consider staying an extra half day to help accomplish some of the administrative tasks that are necessary when your child moves away from home. This will allow you, as a parent, to leave campus secure in the knowledge that your student has everything in place to allow him/her to focus on making new friends and experiencing all of the fun events planned before school actually starts.

If your student doesn't already have a computer of their own, or if it is outdated or a bit tired, take advantage of the discounts that colleges give to incoming students. We ordered computers for both of our kids at orientation, or soon after, with the information their schools provided. Not only did we get a great discount, but by purchasing it through the university, the computer automatically came with free tech support for as long as they were enrolled in the college and included a loaner laptop when their computer needed service. This proved invaluable when one of our kids' computers crashed fall semester and they were able to take it to the Student Union, get a loaner, and have it fixed within days. We never even heard about it until after the fact; that's how smoothly everything worked! The computers were even sent to our home over the summer so our kids had plenty of time to set them up and "move in" to the new hardware well before school started. One more thing to get done in advance to reduce your student's anxiety, and your own.

While most college students bring their own bikes from home, sometimes it is infeasible due to distance or the type of bike your student will need. Orientation is a great time to pick out a bike at a local shop. If you attend a summer orientation, you can even have the bike shop hold it until you return in the fall (which they are more than happy to do if you pay for it in advance.)

On urban campuses, an inexpensive, single-speed bike is best so it doesn't attract the attention of thieves. Just remember to purchase fenders for rainy days, to help your student avoid getting soaked on his/her way to class. On a more confined college campus, you will find an exponential number of beach cruiser bikes, in every color of the rainbow. This is the preferred mode of transportation for girls who don't already have their own mountain bike. Not only does our daughter use her beach cruiser daily to get from one side of campus to another in a timely manner, she even named her bike – she loves it that much.

Lastly, if your child is attending an out-of-state school, he/she will likely need to set up a checking account, especially if the state does not have the same bank where you typically do business at home. Most banks in college towns are very student-friendly and often offer no-fee, no-minimum-balance checking accounts. At one of the schools we attended for orientation, a local bank had advisors in mobile kiosks in the Student Union so we could set up the account literally while sitting on campus, without ever walking into the bank. Remember to be a co-signer on the account so you can send funds electronically to your student's account from your bank account, or theirs, at home. I was thrilled to learn that an electronic funds transfer (EFT) can now go between banks as long as you are also named on the account with your child.

Dorm Options: Living and Learning Communities

After your child has committed to the college of his/her choice, and often before orientation, they will be contacted by the Residence Life department about selecting housing. Depending on the university, a multitude of dormitory options abound. From girls-only or boys-only floors to suite-style rooms, which means two or more rooms separated by a bathroom, to co-ed floors that share a common bathroom, the possibilities are endless. This is yet another reason to attend the college's Admitted Student Days; it can help your student visualize the different housing options and decide his/her preferred choice.

Living and Learning Communities (LLCs) deserve special mention to clarify exactly what the intriguing acronym means. These are dorms that house students of similar majors – think Engineering, Business, or even the Honors College. Generally speaking, LLCs boast some of the newer dorms, are usually just a few steps away from a new or renovated dining hall, many have classrooms on the main floor, and even offer activities for the whole dorm to participate in, which are entirely optional. Our daughter chose to live in the Natural Science Living and Learning Community, which meant that everyone in her dorm was a declared Biology, Pre-Med, Zoology, or any other type of Natural Science major. The bonus to living in these communities is that your student will live with kids who take some of the same classes, making for easy study groups. Also, to be completely honest, the facilities are some of the nicest on campus – think bigger rooms, newer bathrooms, and in some cases in-room HVAC, including dorm-wide air conditioning.

The only catch to being able to live in an LLC is that students have to fill out an application, which often includes one or more essays articulating why he/she wants to live in such a place. In our daughter's case, she had to write three different essays to get into her LLC, but she will tell you it was worth it to live in a new building with like-minded students, elevators, coveted air conditioning, and a specific study space including hammocks, a fireplace, and a living plant wall. Yes, college has changed quite a bit in the last few years.

Finding a Roommate

Once your student's housing is set, next comes the inevitable question – what about a roommate? My best advice on this subject: let your student take the lead, but encourage him/her to find a roommate rather than having the college select a "random roommate." These words alone explain why this could potentially be the downfall of your student's freshman year, especially when colleges today are so savvy about getting potential roommates connected via technology.

Most universities have private Facebook accounts to help match up roommates. Think of match.com, but for finding a roommate. Your student will answer a series of questions about their living style – if they're neat or not, a night owl or an early riser, what their interests are, religious orientation, etc. Then the app gives your student a list of names of people that are a potential match and he/she can contact them on the private

Facebook account and start to "get to know them." This is great because it takes the guesswork out of whether or not your child and her roommate will have anything in common and helps them coordinate who is bringing what to the dorm room.

Once your student has selected a roommate and Residence Life has confirmed they are paired together, it is a great idea to see if you can meet up with them before school starts, at either orientation or on your way to/from orientation. Again this eases the uncertainty of who your child will be living with for the next year, not only for your student, but for you, as parents, as well.

What Do They Really Need to Take to College?

Your student's orientation folder will include a checklist of all of the required things they will need for college, as well as some "nice to haves," his/her dorm set up, and meal plans that he/she has chosen.

In reality, college freshmen only need the basics – a computer, bed linens, towels, toiletries, clothes, and a few things to put on the walls to make their room more personal and less sterile. Yes, even guys will want to add some color to their white concrete, or if they're lucky, dry-walled surroundings. And while you may think the latest LED light-string trend is just for girls, I've seen plenty of guys decorate their rooms with Christmas lights and leave them up the rest of the year. Just don't make the mistake of calling the boy's version "fairy lights," as my son strongly corrected me on multiple occasions.

One of the things I underestimated was the importance of was a memory foam mattress topper. Our daughter made selecting one her first priority, even before the color and design of her comforter, which for girls sets the whole décor of the room. Our son, however, did not see the need for a mattress topper, and within his first week on campus, he had purchased one. These soft, cushy mattress accoutrements come completely compressed, so they are easy to pack for move-in, yet expand to full size and make kids feel like they are sleeping on a real mattress, not one that has been slept on by countless students before them. Remember the fairy tale of the Princess and the Pea? Enough said.

In addition to these necessities, a microwave and/or refrigerator can make dorm life a little more comfortable. Students can eat breakfast in their rooms or reheat whatever dinner they grab on their way home from a night class. We tried both of the possible scenarios – the rentable combination micro-fridge from the college itself, and the other alternative where one roommate purchases a mini fridge and the other a microwave. I highly recommend the former option, since both appliances are already in your student's dorm room when you arrive, and despite many parent's concerns they come impeccably clean. The other bonus of the college rental unit is that both appliances are smaller than most standard mini refrigerators and microwaves, since the appliances come stacked on top of each other. This is essential if your child is living on an urban campus where dorm rooms are tiny, or in any dormitory built back in the '50s that hasn't been updated to suite style. It also saves the inevitable question at the end of the school year: we now have an extra microwave, what are we going to do with it, and do we really have to move it back home?

Last but not least, be prepared for the fact that different kids, and the location of the school, will require different ways to get all of their "stuff" to campus. Since our son was attending an urban college halfway across the country, and we were flying there to move him in, he managed to pack everything he needed into a mere three duffel bags. Before you expect this to be true of every college student, keep in mind that we planned to purchase some of the larger items such as portable storage bins, food, and a fan once we were in the city itself. Additionally, our son elected to purchase all of his linens from a program offered through the university's bookstore, so all he had to do was walk to the dormitory across from his and pick up his sheets, comforter, pillow, and towels on move-in day. So all he really needed to pack were his clothes.

Since our daughter was attending a school located just a few states away from home, and we were able to drive to move her in, she had a lot more latitude with the amount of things that she took with her to college. And let's be honest, girls have an entirely different vision of how they want their dorm rooms to look. Unlike her brother, she selected her own linens via a combination of online shopping and multiple trips to Target. She also found a more permanent storage solution to plastic bins via what we affectionately called the "cubie thing," which housed nine separate cubby holes with fabric storage containers. It was darling, albeit with "some assembly required."

As is common with most girls, our daughter had twice the amount of clothes and shoes as her brother, along with cute knickknacks for décor, and a lamp and bookshelf for her desk, which her school didn't provide, but his did. Instead of unrealistically assuming that we could fit everything into our car, and since her brother was helping move her in so that all four seats were occupied, we ended up renting a Suburban, amid significant protests from our daughter. And you know what? Every single thing fit. Without any room to spare.

CHAPTER THREE

Saying Goodbye – Let Your Child Be Your Guide

If you skipped the first two chapters and started reading this one, no worries. Chances are, if the tables were turned, I would have done the same thing. Or saved this chapter until the very last because of my head-in-the-sand mentality since both of my kids were leaving for college at the exact same time. Regardless of what order you choose to read this book, just know I've been there, and was given great advice by two highly respected therapists. And while it was hard, really hard, the whole process went as smoothly as possible because of some careful planning.

Let's be honest. You've probably been visualizing saying goodbye to your student at college since they started the application process. Whether your image includes a tearful farewell on the steps of an ivy-covered, beautifully architected dormitory, or a hug that lasts for days under leafy trees on the prettiest part of campus, it's time to let the fantasy go. The best way to say goodbye to your young adult is to let him/her decide when and where this big moment (for all of you) occurs.

As the Dean at one of the colleges our kids attended wisely professed, "There will be no last supper, since there was only one true Last Supper, which was with Jesus and his disciples." His point was that most parents have grandiose plans of moving their student into his/her dorm room and then taking them out to dinner for a final goodbye. While this makes perfect sense as a parent, I can assure you that your college freshman has a totally different view of how this day should go down. Their vision likely involves you dropping off their belongings and giving you a quick hug goodbye while they rush off with their new hall mates/roommate to one of the many "Welcome" events planned for freshmen. If this gives you goosebumps, read on to learn how you can still enjoy a private goodbye with your child. Without requiring them to indulge in a last supper.

Ask Them What They Want

Before my twins went to college, I was already in the midst of a pretty intense depression and had been in therapy for a year and a half. It all started when my father passed away from complications of diabetes, having his right leg amputated, and then refusing to let the surgeons take his only remaining leg after it became infected. I was an only child.

Such was the lead-in to my kids' senior year in high school. My brilliant therapist, a strong Christian like myself, reminded me that, just like letting Dad go was part of the circle of life, letting my kids go was part of the circle of parenting. If we do our job as parents, it means sending our child off into the real world with confidence, so he/she can blossom into the adult we couldn't even begin to fathom when we first held them in our arms. All this is to say that, if I, in my heightened emotional state, could have a positive goodbye with my college student, then you can too.

As the weeks approaching move-in grew closer, my therapist started guiding me on what to expect when my twins were "left" at their respective colleges. She wisely suggested asking each of them how they would prefer to say goodbye, since being different kids, they both probably had different visions of what the farewell would look like.

My daughter was the first to leave, so I asked what she preferred for the Big Day, since she would be saying goodbye to not only my husband and me, but also her twin brother, who was helping move her into her dorm. This would be the first time they had been separated for more than a few weeks, and they would literally be across the country from each other.

The first thing my daughter, who is a sweet, kind, and sensitive soul, said was, "I really don't want you guys to stay for Welcome Week," even though parents were invited to participate in the first few days. While we were a little taken aback at her honesty, and quite frankly surprised at her request, I actually felt an instant sense of relief that we wouldn't be hanging around, dragging out the goodbye process. And her rationale was solid: she knew she needed time to meet new friends and get integrated into campus life without worrying about entertaining her parents. Very mature, I thought, with a mixture of both pride and nausea.

Since we knew it would take some time to get all of her belongings unpacked so her dorm room felt like home, we suggested taking her out to breakfast the next day, since she had activities planned with her Living and Learning Community starting at 4 p.m. the day of move-in. If nothing else, my girl loves breakfast. She jumped at the invitation.

Our son, as expected, had a very different vision of what his goodbye should look like. He was more of the mindset that we would move him in within a few hours and he would spend the rest of the day with his roommate and newfound friends on the swim team. It was much more of the "drop and go" mentality, which was not totally unexpected from a guy. I made my peace with it, only to be pleasantly surprised when, as we were walking to meet our daughter's roommate and her family for lunch on the day we all moved her in, he said, "A last lunch might be nice." Cue fireworks and rockets in my mind, while on the outside I tried to maintain a calm, cool demeanor and merely said, "We can do that." And so the plans were set.

There Will Be Tears – How to Handle Them

Soon the fateful day arrived and we were moving our daughter into her beautiful, brand new dormitory.

As we walked into her room for the first time, I felt an instant sense of dread. This would be her home for the next nine months, meaning she wouldn't be nestled in her cozy bed in the room she had slept in since she was five years old, which was only a floor away from ours, and under the same roof. I took a deep breath and helped her start organizing.

Many hours later, everything was in place. Her bed was made, complete with the brand new comforter, sheets, and fluffy throw pillows we had so carefully picked out together in the months leading up to this moment. Fairy lights were hung, illuminating pictures of family and friends which were attached with clothespins so the wall next to her bed looked like something from a Pinterest board. Mementos from her 12 years of dance were carefully placed on the bookshelf above her desk, along with a framed picture of her and her twin brother, given to her by a friend as a graduation gift. With a knot in my stomach, we hugged her, told her to have fun planting succulents and tie-dyeing at her dorm party, and promised to see her in the morning. At which point, my thoughtful daughter said, "Mom, I want to leave it up to you where we say goodbye after breakfast. Do you want me to meet you at the restaurant or do you want to pick me up, so you can drop me back off, here at the dorm?" Instantly, the vision of saying goodbye to my baby girl in the parking lot of the Waffle Lab popped into my mind and seemed sterile and asphalt-ridden. So I told her we would pick her up and that was that.

The next morning I woke with an ache in my heart and shed a few tears while my husband said a prayer. Then we woke our son, who was snoring in the bed next to us. Holding back tears, I showered and got dressed while putting on the minimal amount of makeup – certainly no mascara. Breakfast was a blur, but we all knew it was a chance to relish the last time the four of us would be together until Thanksgiving, which seemed like light years away from that warm August day.

After breakfast we pulled up to the dorm and I asked my reluctant daughter for a picture of the four of us on the lawn outside, something we would repeat with my son when we moved him in a few weeks later. Then it was time. She hugged me first and the tears came immediately, plentiful but welcome as I held her close and wished I never had to let go. Then she hugged my husband and he whispered some soothing, wise words to her while tearing up himself. Next, it was her twin brother's turn. Standing at six feet one inches, he would have passed for her big brother rather than a twin, which was sort of true since he was born a minute earlier. In that moment a little piece of my heart broke, like the Grinch but in reverse, and then the three of us climbed into the car while she walked away. I alternated between crying and sleeping during the eight-hour car ride home. My husband kept patting my leg, in part to let me know that it was all going to be okay and also, I think, to remind himself that we were in this together.

In the blink of an eye, which was actually only a few weeks later, we were back at it again, moving our son into his high-rise dorm in the middle of a city. And yet, the whole experience was different. A five-hour plane ride meant he had to pack all of his belongings into a series of overstuffed duffel bags, then we took an Uber from our hotel to his dorm to move him in.

Still, the feelings were the same. When a bunch of guys from the swim team ducked their heads into the room as we were unloading and invited him to join them for a swim, he politely declined, much to my relief. I tried to be a grown-up by telling him it was okay if we skipped our goodbye lunch, so he could swim with his new teammates, but he insisted he wanted to get everything unpacked first. Which resulted in a huge, internal sigh of relief on my part.

While he had far fewer photos to decorate his wall than his sister, our son hung exactly eight of them over his desk. One of the four of us, one of each of his good friends, and two of our dog. With his gifted sense of humor, my son remarked that this proved he would miss our white, furry, poodle/bichon mix most of all. He carefully placed the same framed picture of his twin sister and himself, which he had also received for graduation, on his desk and my heart once again dropped. Then it was time for lunch, which went by way too fast.

Afterwards, we asked someone to take a picture of the three of us beneath a tree standing in the beautifully landscaped area in front of his dorm. As we started to hug, I panicked, realizing I hadn't prepared some meaningful piece of advice to impart. Just when I was about to feel inadequate as a parent, he hugged me back with all his might and said, "I'm going to miss you so much! Thanks for letting me come to school here." At which point the tears began to flow. Again. Just as I was on the verge of a full-blown ugly cry, his teammates walked out of the dorm behind us. I pulled away and insisted he join them – even though they were most likely headed to get something to eat after their swim. Never mind the fact that he had just eaten lunch with us. At first he resisted, but with one more hug, and a promise to call every Sunday, he turned and joined them while I shouted to his teammates, "He's all yours now – take good care of him."

This time, there wasn't the luxury of climbing into our own car and curling up into a ball to let the tears flow.

So my kind husband slowly guided me to a bench on the other side of the dorm, held me in his arms, and let me sob uncontrollably. When I finally composed myself, we both looked up to see my son and his new friends walking down the street in front of us, toward the local pizza joint. It was truly a God thing, since our bench was tucked under a tree away from the street. This meant we could see him but he didn't see us, which was just fine. My last memory of dropping our only son off at college was him walking away with his friends into a big, bright future.

Another Family's Goodbye

To demonstrate that not all families are the same, just as not all kids are the same, it helps to get some perspective from another mom's "goodbye story." While the circumstances are different, the feelings are glaringly similar. In hindsight, I wish I had heard this story before we left each of our kids at college. It certainly would have made me feel more normal about my reactions and feelings at the time.

Kristen still had one son in high school when her oldest left for college. She recalls that watching the boys say goodbye to each other was by far the hardest part for her. The next hardest part was actually leaving her eldest at college. Since his orientation was the day before move-in, she remembers walking around campus holding onto the orientation schedule for dear life since it helped her feel like she knew where her freshman was each and every moment.

When the time finally came to say goodbye, Kristen admits, "I was a total wreck. He was walking away from us, and my husband and I started to bawl. We literally ran to the car, closed and locked the doors, and cried for 20 minutes. I don't think we said a word the whole way home."

So what's the lesson in all of these tear-invoking memories? Even though it is a good idea to keep your emotions in check during move-in, and not cry every time you unpack their favorite sweater or photos, it's perfectly okay to allow the tears to flow when you say goodbye. Your kids are expecting it, from both their parents, and so should you. Just try your best not to break down into the full ugly cry until they've walked away.

Self-Care Once You Are Back Home

This probably sounds silly, but in the first few weeks of my kids being away at college, it literally felt like they'd been gone forever. I stayed in bed for as long as possible in the mornings, dreading the absence of a routine which had evolved over the last 18 years. I cried whenever I opened the refrigerator or pantry, seeing their favorite foods staring back at me, none of which my husband or I would eat. In one rather absurd moment, opening the refrigerator and seeing my daughter's favorite lemonade-flavored coconut water brought me to tears. When I asked my husband how it got there, he told me he had bought it for himself as post-workout hydration. I irrationally replied, "Then keep it downstairs in the bar fridge where I can't see it!"

Thankfully, I'm blessed to be married to a man who has the patience of a saint, and after giving me a big hug, he quietly moved the coconut water out of sight and handed me a Kleenex. Side note – it only took until after the kids were home for Christmas break for coconut water to be "allowed" in the kitchen refrigerator again without causing fits of tears every time I saw it.

When the pantry and refrigerator contents weren't causing emotional reactions, I was doing a stellar job of avoiding my college-aged kids' bedrooms. It took at least a week, after my daughter and then son moved out, before I dared to climb the rustic wood stairs to their rooms for fear of crawling under their bed covers and never coming out. When I did get up the nerve to embark on the trek upstairs, everything felt the same as when they had been home, but also completely different. Empty from their absence. I found myself missing the days of clothes, books, backpacks, and the errant lunch bag strewn across the carpet. You might not be able to fathom this, especially if you have multiple offspring still at home, but one day you, too, will miss it.

A few weeks into my grieving period, the rational side of my brain kicked in. Or, more likely, daily devotionals, long talks with my husband, church sermons, and therapy made me realize my kids weren't dead, they were "only" away at college. Snicker all you want, that having a child in college felt like the equivalent of the loss of a loved one, but that is exactly what my irrational mama bear mind experienced whenever I came home to an empty house.

The key to getting through those first few weeks, or months, when your child is away at college is to practice lots of self-care. Does this mean drinking a bottle of wine all by yourself as you sniffle on the couch? Absolutely not, although nobody would fault you if you did. But you would feel worse the next morning anyway.

Self-care means listening to your body and finding what gives you peace. For some people it means taking a nap, or treating yourself to a massage or pedicure to help you relax. It could mean completely immersing yourself in a new book, binge-watching Netflix, or meeting a friend for coffee to talk about how you're feeling...or talk about nothing at all. Yoga and exercise are also great outlets, as long as you can focus on being totally in the moment and not let your mind wander into missing your kids. As a matter of fact, self-care can mean something different every day, or even every hour of the week.

I can recall lying on the couch one Saturday afternoon, cocooned under a soft, fuzzy blanket and alternately napping, watching TV, and observing individual flakes of snow fall outside our living room window. Just about every hour I'd check in with myself and ask, "What does my body need right now?" and the answer kept coming back the same. I just needed to rest, forget my to-do list, and just be. On that couch, under that blanket – safe, warm, and content.

CHAPTER FOUR

BUILDING A STRONG MARRIAGE

Long before orientation, and certainly before you send your child off to college, do yourself, your family, and your spouse a favor and start strengthening your marriage. At this point, you've likely been married for a while. And let's be honest, you probably aren't in the newlywed stage anymore. Marriage is hard. Raising kids is hard. Put the two together, and you get a double whammy. The last thing you want after you drop your first or last child at college is to get back in the car and look at each other wondering, "Who are you?"

Think of your marriage like your body. To stay strong it needs to be in shape, which means building strength between the two of you; bulking up your bond like a body builder. To be happily married for a lifetime requires commitment, diligence, and iron-clad barriers to outside influences that can make your bond weaker. The goal is to be stronger together than apart.

Does this mean forsaking all else such as individual friendships, hobbies, and interests in favor of your spouse? Not at all. But it does mean being intentional in the months leading up to high school graduation and starting to imagine living your life without your college student at the center of it.

Why Is Strengthening Your Marriage Important?

We've all heard the stories – Johnny gets dropped off for his freshman year of college by both parents and comes home at the holidays only to be told they're getting a divorce. Or worse, they are already divorced. One of them has moved out and the poor kid is told his parents can no longer afford to send him to the expensive university, where he just completed his first semester, because they have to pay for two separate places to live. Heartbreaking.

While this is the far end of the spectrum, it isn't unusual for spouses to leave their child at college and wonder, what comes next? The answer can range from new careers to traveling to starting a hobby you've always wanted to try. But it can also mean realizing you've both changed, a lot, during the years that you've been focused on raising successful, young adults who have moved onto the next phase of their lives. Maybe it's time for you two to get to know each other. Again.

One couple, Cindy and Darren, mentioned in Chapter One, were introduced to a marriage class, called Two Becoming One, after both of their daughters moved away. It is a faith-based course that they found through their church in another state and brought with them when they moved to our town. According to Cindy, "We have been teaching it every year since we took the class ourselves, since it rocked our world so much and really helped us with the relationship with our kids. Now we even do mentoring, along with the class, and our marriage has just gotten better and better. It really strengthened us by helping with the transition of not having kids at home."

The truth is, when your child goes to college you will miss them, and you will go through a period of grieving over the fact that they no longer live at home. You may feel lonely at times. Isolated. Stuck. And it is in this moment you may hit a critical juncture in your marriage. Are you going to handle this transition together, holding each other up when you're struggling? Or are you going to white knuckle it on your own and come out on the other side, stronger as an individual, but not necessarily more connected with your spouse? The good news is you don't have to go it alone. With some focused time and effort before your child leaves home, and immediately after, you and your spouse can emerge from this somewhat scary transition, stronger as individuals with a renewed marriage that brings both of you closer than before.

Weekly Date Nights

About six months after our twins were born, my husband and I went to see a couple's therapist, since we were having trouble connecting; physically, mentally, and emotionally. While twins are double blessings from God, they also intensify the newborn process two-fold, and both my husband and I had no energy left for each other.

The first suggestion from our therapist, a loving, kind Christian mother of four, was to go on weekly date nights. My immediate, unfiltered response was, "Are you kidding me? I don't have the time or energy for date night! Let alone the fact that just the thought of getting dressed up makes me feel exhausted."

Instead, we decided on date days, realizing my husband and I would have more energy during the day than we would come dinnertime. Plus, it gave us the chance to exercise and be outdoors, something we both enjoyed. It worked for a while, but our date days became less and less consistent over the years, especially as the kids got older and had different activities on the weekends, forcing us to go in separate directions, each with one twin. Before we knew it, our date days were once a month, at best.

Fast forward to fall of our kids' senior year. My dad had passed away eight months earlier and I was back in therapy – for myself this time. While helping me work through the grief that comes from losing a parent, my new therapist wisely counseled me to turn to my husband as a source of support. She also suggested that now was the time to refocus on our marriage, so that together we were strong when the kids moved out. Guess what the first thing she proposed was? Weekly date nights. Again.

This time I didn't fight it, remembering the benefits of our date days many years prior, back when the kids were toddlers and in elementary school. And to be perfectly honest, if a different therapist in a different state was giving me the same advice, chances were it was God's way of telling me to listen this time.

Since our kids were both driving, it was easy to come up with a night during the week when they were at their respective activities so my husband and I could go out to dinner. It also saved me from cooking one night, which was a blessing in and of itself. At first, we made sure there were leftovers for the twins to heat up before or after swimming and dance, but once they figured out we would pay for takeout, they handled their dinner in a collaborative way. In the morning, on their way to school, they'd decide what they wanted to eat for dinner and my son would pick it up on his way home from swimming. They would eat at the bar in our kitchen together while we headed out to our restaurant of choice. It all worked seamlessly, until one week when we changed date night from Tuesday to Wednesday. After we got home from dinner that night, our daughter informed us that Tuesdays were the only days that worked for her, since her brother could deliver their food in enough time for her to eat before she was due at the dance studio. My husband and I chuckled and happily left date night on Tuesday, a tradition we've continued to honor even now when they're off at college.

So what is the benefit of a weekly date night? First, whether it's on a Tuesday or a Saturday, a night out together gives you the chance to step away from the nightly grind of making dinner to accommodate multiple kids and their activities that inevitably occur at different times. If you have younger kids, enlist the help of your high school senior to drive them to their activities. This gives you the added bonus of getting a night off not only as the chef, but also the chauffeur.

Second, date night gives you and your spouse a chance to connect and talk without the distractions of kids, laundry, dishes, and yes, technology. The number one rule of date night – put your phones away in your purse or a pocket, leaving just one ringer on in case a child needs you, and talk to each other instead of catching up on emails or social media. A weekly one- or even two-hour technology break can make a significant difference in your marriage, trust me.

Third, you need to remember that date night is about you and your spouse, so try to limit the amount of time you talk about your kids. Yes, one of them is leaving for college in less than a year, and with that comes many parental conversations, but the purpose of date night is to spend time together, talking about each other's needs, and your goals and dreams once your kids are out of the house. Use this time to brainstorm places you'd like to travel or organizations you'd like to join or volunteer for when you have more free time. Talk about your careers and where you see them going in the next few years while you're paying for college tuition. If one of you hasn't been in the workforce for a while, brainstorm the type of job he/she would enjoy pursuing and come up with a plan together to make it happen. If one of you is dissatisfied at work, talk about options in terms of alternative jobs, lighter hours, or the ability to work from home. Use this time to map out what your individual lives and your married life will look and feel like once the house is empty, or emptier.

Does weekly date night mean you have to shell out hundreds of dollars to go to a fancy restaurant, get dressed up, and eat fancy food? Absolutely not. It can be as simple as using a coupon or even picking an inexpensive place that is a family favorite, but just going by yourselves this time. It can mean packing a picnic and finding a secluded spot where the two of you can sit, talk, and enjoy nature. Date night doesn't have to be expensive or elaborate. What it does need to be is time carved out, every week or every other week, for just you and your spouse. The added benefit is that it will show your kids that you're putting effort into spending time together, which will ease any subconscious concerns they may have about your marriage being stable once they leave for college.

Romantic Weekends Away

While weekly date nights are a great way to connect mentally and emotionally with your spouse, there is still the important element of making time to connect physically as well. Even though you have high schoolers, who spend more time away from home than younger kids, there is still a constant revolving door of activity that makes it difficult to spend romantic evenings at home. And let's be honest, sex is a very important part of marriage. It's God's gift to us, which started way back in the Garden of Eden with Adam and Eve, but can naturally wax and wane during the years we're raising children.

At the beginning of our kids' senior year of high school, we discovered a crack in our marriage that showed both of us how important it is to continue to connect romantically. So we sought out a couple's therapist to help us reconnect. Yes, this means that during my kids' senior year, and into the next when they were away at school, I was in therapy for two sessions a week, every week – one with my individual therapist and the other with our couple's therapist. Without a doubt, it was my faith in God and the help of those two amazing counselors that allowed me to enjoy my kids' senior year, prepared me for saying goodbye to them, and gave my husband and me the gift of a new and improved marriage in which we became closer than ever before.

So guess what the couple's therapist's first suggestion was? Not more date nights, but something very similar. Romantic weekends away, just the two of us. The thought of luxuriating under the covers in a hotel room with my husband, waking without an alarm, and enjoying a hot breakfast made by somebody else sounded lovely, soothing, and peaceful. Just what the doctor ordered.

Luckily we live in the same town as my mother, who was more than happy to come stay with the kids while we ventured to a local resort only 45 minutes from home, which felt like a world away. Unfortunately for my mom, she spent more quality time with our dog than her grandchildren, who came and went at all times of the day. Still, because she was there, we knew they were well-fed and not having parties in our absence −

something that did happen the one time we left them alone for a weekend, after which Grammy was commissioned to stay for all future occasions when we went away. This was confirmation to us that nobody's kids are perfect, and high schoolers will be rebellious, given the chance.

There is something inherently romantic about getting away for the weekend, just the two of you, and either exploring a new area or reacquainting yourself with an old favorite. We chose locations that allowed us to hike or ski, and reveled in the lack of structure and being able to set our own schedule, often not deciding where we would eat dinner until four in the afternoon.

If you have the ability to go to a fancy hotel or even fly to another city for the weekend, then by all means take advantage of it. If finances are tight, which is perfectly understandable since you are preparing to start paying hefty college tuition for the next four years, then get creative with where you stay. VRBO and Airbnb have great options at affordable prices, and will allow you to get away while staying in a home or apartment so you can prepare most of your own meals, possibly treating yourself to the occasional dinner or lunch at a restaurant. Alternatively, many hotel chains now include breakfast in the price and even have microwaves and refrigerators in the rooms. The point is, don't disregard the chance of a romantic weekend away because of cost or time. The benefits are so great, to you and your spouse – mentally, spiritually, emotionally, and physically – that these respites are a crucial step in preparing for your empty nest.

Finding Mentors

One of the things my husband and I didn't realize, until sometime around our kids' junior year in high school, was how we rarely spent time with other couples, with the exception of swim meets or dance competitions. And even these encounters involve hastily eating fast food in between sessions or sitting next to other parents in the bleachers talking about our kids and how they were doing in their specific sports. And when we weren't at our kids' activities, we just wanted to stay home, pull on our comfy sweats, cuddle up on the couch, and watch a movie or favorite TV show. If we were lucky, at least one of our kids was around on these kinds of nights, and we could enjoy time with them without really "doing" anything.

Since our house was also the gathering place for our son's friends, we didn't feel right about going out to dinner or an event with another couple when we had a houseful of boys. Not that they'd ever do anything mischievous. Except for the time we caught them playing basketball by standing on the side of the deck, a full 12 feet over the driveway, and trying to get the ball in the basket by throwing it over the back board. Or the many times the ball rolled down the hill (read cliff) and they bushwhacked through scrub oak on a 60-degree slope to retrieve it.

So when their senior year arrived, we just accepted the fact that time with other couples would take a backseat to our parenting and we would pick it up after the kids were gone. Once again, our couple's therapist pointed us in the right direction. He reminded us of the importance of each of us cultivating relationships with other empty nesters who could help mentor us through the next few years.

I sought out a few women from our church with grown married children and who shared the same parenting philosophy as me. We would meet for coffee every few months and I would pick their brains about what to expect for the remainder of high school, the summer before college, and then the dreaded saying goodbye. They lovingly and happily listened to my fears and concerns and provided wisdom for which I am still grateful to this day.

One of those women, Laurel, told me that she and her husband started a tradition after all three of her kids left for college. They purposely sit down at the table and have dinner together every night they're home, just the two of them. "My husband will say that is his favorite thing about being empty nesters. We sit down without TV or phones and just have dinner together. We both really look forward to it," she recounted with a smile.

While I was reaching out to mentors, my husband did the same with his circle of friends, connecting with a couple of guys he knew who had kids in college. While they would sometimes meet for coffee, they'd often go biking together and the guys would ask how our kids were dealing with choosing a college or finishing out their final season of high school sports, and they'd check in with how my husband was feeling about it all.

To this day, these kind men and women are the first to ask us how our kids are doing at their respective colleges, and still provide insights on how to deal with letting our young adults grow a little more independent with each passing year.

Cultivating Couple Time with Others

Admittedly, one of the things we still need to work on in our marriage is cultivating friendships with other couples. By the second semester of our twins' freshman year in college, we had strengthened each other and our marriage so well that we felt ready to branch out and find other couples to do things with. However, two problems arose.

First, if we tried to spend time with couples whose kids were still in school, scheduling time around their busy lives was difficult, to say the least. And, when we finally would settle on a date, our busy friends basically had an hour or so to grab a quick bite to eat before they had to rush home and tend to their teenagers and younger kids. We made the most of this by going out for a drink or dessert afterwards, just the two of us, so we had the added benefit of spending couple time with others while enjoying a partial date night to ourselves. Still, even though we weren't envious of their crazy lives, we found it a challenge to adjust to our newly wide-open schedules.

If we tried to spend time with other empty nesters, a different problem arose. Couples without kids at home travel a lot more, ourselves included. So it was much easier to fall into the trap of spending our weekends at home, just the two of us, instead of branching out to others in the same stage of life.

One solution to this was deciding to take on a hobby together, in hopes of meeting other like-minded couples. We joined the local wine tasting club, and while we had a great time, no real couple friendships emerged, since most of the folks in the club were much older than us. Still, we looked forward to the monthly events, where we focused on learning the art of wine tasting and being educated about the different soils and regions of wine rather than making lifelong friendships.

One mom, Kristen, who I mentioned in Chapter Three, was lucky enough to know 10-12 other moms with their first child going off to college in the same year, so she creatively organized a celebratory cocktail party for all of them once the kids were all gone. While she didn't do it in a couple's format, the same concept could apply. She invited all the women over to her house and they stood in a circle in her kitchen and laughed and cried. Everyone reported on their collegians – who was happy, who was sad, who was texting, who wasn't. There was joy for them in "just talking and not feeling so alone, with a lot of laughter and shared ideas," she said. After the event, this same group of women morphed into an impromptu support group whereby the moms would text or email each other just to check-in. One of the guests even brought a quote to the party about giving your kids wings to fly, which morphed into this endearing symbol of flapping arms like wings – a motion they would exchange when they saw each other around town, at the grocery store, or running errands.

Support from fellow mothers is important, especially since some husbands get annoyed that, even though the kids are gone, their wife might not necessarily pour all of her attention on him. Yet another reason to find other empty nester couples to share time with: so that the husbands can better understand what the wives are going through, and vice versa, via shared stories among the group.

CHAPTER FIVE

Staying in Touch – Ask What Works for Them

Before you say your final goodbyes, it's important to come up with a plan, even if it is just for the first few weeks of school, of how often and what method you will use to communicate with your student. Why can't you just call or text them whenever you want? While you certainly can, it's best to give your young adult the time and space they need to immerse themselves in their new world, without worrying about checking in with you.

Does this mean radio silence for the first few weeks they are at college? Absolutely not. That's not healthy for either party. They need to know they can contact you whenever they want, and you need to have a general idea of when to expect them to reach out, so you have something to look forward to.

Our family started out using the old-fashioned, tried-and-true, "Call your mother every Sunday," approach. This goes back to ancient times, when we were in college, and would call our parents every Sunday night using the corded phone attached to a wall in either our dorm room or sorority/fraternity house.

Given that it had been over three decades since this college ritual was recognized as the norm, we soon discovered the pitfalls of the mandated phone calls home, especially when I was looking at the clock every Sunday after church and wondering when each of our twins was going to call. If for some reason they didn't, it would put me in a funk for the next day or two until they actually did call or text. And yes, I'm aware that phones today work both ways, just as they did when we were in college, but I wanted to respect my kids' privacy and not be the needy mom, always calling them first.

Reality check – it's perfectly fine to call your child at college. You are, after all, paying for their tuition. And most importantly, just because they're living away from home doesn't mean you've lost your right to be a parent. Plus, you may find one of your children takes it personally when you don't call them occasionally. Or worse, when you do make a phone call instead of sending a text, they assume you're delivering bad news. So be an example to your kids by actually using your phone to call and talk to them in person. They may not always be able to talk at that moment, if they're in class or studying for an exam, but they'll be happy you reached out. Even if it is what they consider an outdated form of communication.

How Much Is Too Much?

So what is the right amount of time to communicate with your college student? To be honest, it's a fine line that is completely dependent on your child. Some friends of ours dropped their kids off at college and told them they could call whenever they wanted, but kindly asked them to text once a day, just to check in. This worked for the first few weeks for their family, but when my kids heard this scenario their eyes grew wide with an unspoken plea which could only have been translated as, "Please don't make us do that!"

Another mom, Kristen, asked her eldest son to Skype every Sunday since, as she put it, "It was important for me to see him," wisely adding, "You can take one look at your own kid and know if they are getting sick or didn't get enough sleep." To have this ritual every Sunday night or afternoon was important for her. When her youngest went away to school, she texted him every day since he was a bit more naïve than his older brother, and young for his grade.

The bottom line is this: the fact that God makes each of our children unique and different should give us insight into the best way to communicate with them. Case in point – our daughter would call us a few times a week, often when she was riding her bike back from class alone in the dark (the thought of this still makes my blood run cold) or just to check in and update us on classes, activities, or whatever she had going on at the time. Alternatively, we would only hear from our son during the requisite Sunday phone call, which often consisted of single-word answers. And if we tried to FaceTime him, it resulted in him looking at his computer screen while we were trying to have a conversation.

After the first semester, we rescinded the mandatory Sunday phone calls for both kids. The end result was that our son called when he knew he had the time and was truly interested in talking to us. The outcome was much more engaging, albeit less frequent, communication.

So what did I learn from our attempt at planned communication with our college students? Ask what works for them, and realize it may evolve during the first few weeks and or even the first few months of school. It may even continue to ebb and flow over the next four years. And that's okay. They're still your kids. They still love you and need you. They just need their own space, too.

Alternatives to Phone Calls

Despite technology and all the ways we communicate now, there is something special about hearing your child's voice. Skype and FaceTime are great ways to add the human component to your conversation, by seeing your child's face and being able to visualize them in their new surroundings. It can also be a way to keep them in touch with the feeling of home and how their parents' lives are evolving with them out of the house. We would occasionally FaceTime our kids so they could see our dog when we were at home or where we were staying when we traveled, so they felt part of our new lives in a small way, just like we felt part of theirs. FaceTime was also a useful tool when they wanted things sent from home, so we could physically go into their rooms and get the exact item they needed. We even used it to show the kids when we painted the interior of our house, so they wouldn't come home for a visit and be totally offended by the fact that we had dared to change part of the décor in their childhood home.

It's also important to be open to new technology that may be uncomfortable for parents to adjust to at first, but is a form of communication that your kids use regularly. When we asked our twins how they wanted to stay in touch with us, other than the required weekly phone calls, they both answered the same – Snapchat. Admittedly, during the life of this book, there will be a myriad of other, more hip ways to communicate with your college student without making it burdensome to them, the technology generation. But when we sent our kids off to school, this was their preferred form of communication. Even though it took me awhile to get used to it, I slowly but surely learned how.

At the beginning Snapchat seemed like a silly way to communicate – especially when I'd get Snaps from our son with no caption, which made it feel more like I was playing a Where's Waldo game. For example, during the first week of school he sent me a picture of a marginally empty gym floor with tables set up and a few students milling around in the same college T-shirt. To which I responded, "Did the All Athlete Barbeque get rained out?" Three hours later my son sent me a Snapchat back that was a picture taken from his dorm room of rain pouring down on the soccer field outside his window. Ah, the mystery of Waldo was solved.

Before you think I'm all tech savvy, don't be too impressed. In fact, I still insist to my ever-patient husband that my iPad only charges when it's on and the cover is open, even though he has assured me this is impossible. As far as Snapchat goes, my daughter was extra patient teaching me how to use it. When I learned how to insert captions for the first time, I apparently placed the caption directly across the photo, so she had to Snap me back and ask me to resend it with the caption at the bottom or top. To this day, whenever I see her friends around our hometown and ask them to Snapchat her with me, after being impressed that I'm trying to use the app at all, they usually end up holding the phone at just the right angle and pushing the button themselves. Which has avoided the requisite three or four attempts we'd need if I tried to do it on my own.

Despite my limited Snapchat abilities, I found it easiest to default to texting when a timely answer was needed from my college students. Texting can be a blessing and a curse. First, it's a blessing because kids are much more likely to check Snapchat and text messages before ever answering their phones. So it works like a charm when you need them to confirm dates for a plane flight home that you are researching. However, it can be a curse when your kids use it to query you for information. Since this generation is used to making any form of communication short and sweet, sometimes it can be perplexing to get a rather cryptic text.

One of my favorite examples is when our son texted us, "When did I work last summer?" We assumed he was looking to contact the company he worked for the previous summer, in hopes of returning to work there after his freshman year of college. Other than that, we were stumped. Did he want to know how long he had worked last summer, or was he asking which days of the week he worked, or which shifts? None of these were things we could answer anyway. So my husband did what any parent would do given the lack of information. He called our son to find out exactly what he needed instead of creating a lengthy, and likely frustrating, text exchange.

Regardless of the ways that your family decides to stay in touch while your kids are in college, the important part isn't being proficient in whatever technology they prefer. Rather, it's showing them you're willing to communicate in the way or ways that are most natural or comfortable for them.

One Truly Creative Approach

When Jeanne, mentioned in Chapter Two, sent her youngest off to college, her daughter gave Jeanne a teddy bear and told her mom to hug it whenever she missed her. The youngest of three, this sweet young woman realized her mother would officially be an empty nester and was intuitive enough to understand the intense emotions associated with this stage of life.

Jeanne would hug the bear whenever she missed her daughter. One day when she was talking to her on the phone, she broke down in tears and told her how much she missed her. Her daughter immediately asked if Jeanne had been hugging the teddy bear and if she had felt anything "weird" about the bear. Jeanne replied that it did feel a little hard in the middle, but she just thought that was the only bear her thoughtful girl could afford. Her daughter laughed and told her mom to cut it open along the seam. After arguing about defiling the meaningful stuffed animal, Jeanne finally acquiesced, reached in, and pulled out a framed picture of her and her daughter which had been sewn into the bear. As she cried sweet tears of joy, her daughter told her, "Mom, I love you and I'll always love you." Jeanne recalls with a wistful smile, "It was the sweetest and most healing thing for me. There is a lot of pain when your kids leave and it will never be the same, but to move onto the next chapter, you have to learn to let go."

CHAPTER SIX

Siblings Still at Home – Don't Forget About Them

Even though I had twins, and both of them went to college the same fall, they didn't both leave on the exact same day. In fact, due to different academic calendars, we had two weeks with our son at home after our daughter left. While this is not nearly the same thing as having younger siblings in the house after you've dropped your eldest at college, it did give me a tiny perspective into what it means to have younger siblings you can't ignore, and shouldn't want to. Thankfully, I found quite a few empty nesters with multiple kids of different ages to get their perspective for this chapter on how to approach life at home with one of your kids at college and more yet to get there.

With my son still at home, we felt like parents of an only child for a few weeks, which was good and bad. The good part was that, when he was around, we had him all to ourselves to watch movies, eat dinner, or play video games or foosball. But he really wasn't around much. He was saying his final goodbyes to other high school friends who still hadn't left for college yet either, which dwindled daily since he was one of the last to leave, with move-in over Labor Day weekend. Still, we made the most of our time with him, ticking off things on his summer bucket list, taking him to breakfast at his favorite restaurants, and making sure he had his favorite home-cooked meals. One particularly memorable moment, as mentioned in Chapter One, was when our son and my husband did an overnight backpacking trip to the top of Mt. Timpanogos to see the sunrise, just the two of them. It was something he had always wanted to do and was a particularly poignant memory that both he and my husband will treasure forever.

The downside to just having our son at home was that, after saying goodbye to our daughter in another state, I felt the need to keep my emotions in check so our son wouldn't feel like his mom was falling apart. I certainly didn't want him heading off to his college experience worried about me because of my strong reaction to his sister's departure or concerned that his leaving would exacerbate the problem. So, all that self-care mentioned in Chapter Four happened in private, when he was at work or out with his friends. When he was home, I did my best to keep it together to show that I was going to be okay, despite knowing that I was going to miss him terribly when he was attending school on the other side of the country.

Months later, we heard about another family situation in which the mom totally lost it after her eldest left for college. She and her child were best friends, which was likely part of the problem, since our job as parents isn't to be our child's best friend, but to be their mom or dad. In this woman's case, her lack of self-care and focus on missing her college-aged child made her other kids at home feel inadequate and like they weren't her "favorite." Not a good combination for all involved – the college student, siblings, mom, or dad. So how do you avoid this rather troubling scenario? Read on to see some different parents' perspectives on how to cope when your oldest leaves the nest while you still have a few more ducklings at home.

What It Feels Like

Dropping any of your children at college is hard, but the first one – well that's just downright painful. When Kristen, mother of two, was asked how it felt to leave her oldest, she replied, "Like someone had ripped out a part of my body; it literally felt like someone cut off my arm." She recalls having to put it in perspective and remind himself that her son was only away at college. "I know people who have lost children and they can't text their kid goodnight or ever talk to them again," she said. "I would pull myself out of my pity party, because the reality was I could still pick up the phone and talk to my son." If this sounds a bit melodramatic, it was exactly the same for me. Rational? Not so much. Understandable? Perfectly. After all, you raised this person in your home for 18 years and then poof, he's gone, in what feels like an instant.

Lest you think Kristen and I are in the minority, consider Cindy, whose daughters ended up graduating the same year, even though one was younger, since they both completed high school online. Cindy recalls sitting at their graduation ceremony and suddenly realizing life was going to be very different. "You literally have 18 years to prepare for that day, but for some reason it catches you by surprise. There were moments when I was easing into life after they were gone, and other times when it would blindside me all of a sudden and I would just burst into tears, thinking, where did that come from?"

Her husband confirms this with a tender story that they can now laugh about, years later. The two of them were out on their boat one day after the girls had left home. As they sat back and relaxed, basking in the warmth of the sunshine and the beauty around them, all of a sudden Cindy started to cry. Shocked and concerned, her husband looked at her and asked what was wrong, to which Cindy simply replied, "I miss my girls." Her husband still admits to feeling a combination of relief and confusion, given that she was fine one moment and weeping the next.

After Jeanne, mother of three, dropped her oldest son at college, she remembers the rest of the family really missing his presence at the dinner table. Even though her life was still very full with two high schoolers, she recalls going into her son's room and feeling a mixture of emotions – sadness intertwined with excitement because this was the beginning of his adult life. "I had an overall sense that it would never be the same and he wasn't going to need me the way he used to. I wanted it to be that way, but I didn't. It was hard not knowing what the future of our relationship would be, having an adult child. Because of my faith, I knew God's plans were good, but that didn't mean it would always be easy," she said with tears in her eyes.

Don't Hide Your Grief

One consistent piece of advice I gleaned from all the mothers I've talked to with siblings still at home, was not to try to hide your grief. They mentioned having dinner together with the rest of their kids and husband and talking about how they missed their college student and wondering what he or she was doing at that particular moment in time.

The truth is, everyone in the household feels the ache when a member of the family moves away. But they also know in their hearts that this is the beginning of a new, exhilarating beginning for their son, daughter, brother, or sister. "You hit that season of your life when you realize the chapter of raising kids at home has definitely closed. Those were the times when I felt like I was grieving," says Cindy.

Jeanne recommends also not hiding your grief from yourself. "Face it and deal with it. That will help you be the parent that your children still at home need, since they are dealing with their own grief. If you fall apart in private, or ignore it, then how can your other kids share that they're hurting?"

As mentioned in Chapter Four, this is the part where self-care becomes even more important to you as a mother with siblings still at home. Journaling can be an effective tool to get your feelings out, as well as letting your other kids know how you really feel. "Some moms told me to be joyous for him, but I would talk to his younger brother when I was really missing him and together we would share how weird it felt for him to be gone. That really helped both of us," says Kristen.

Prayer is another tool to make you feel less alone in your grieving and give you the ability to hand over your sorrow, angst, and need to adjust to a new way of parenting. According to Jeanne, "I find what always works best is when I talk to God about it and pour out my heart and get answers and comfort from Him. That makes me more prepared to be who I'm called to be with my husband and all of my kids."

More Advice

Refocusing your energy on your other children is another good coping mechanism for missing your college student – both for you and their siblings. Kristen recalls really enjoying the one-on-one time with her youngest child since it reminded her of the first few years when her eldest was an only child before his little brother came along. "Pouring more energy into my younger son, and giving him his own time to shine, helped me not miss my oldest so much," she recalls.

She also advocates encouraging lots of communication between the sibling who is away and their sister or brother still at home. Kristen constantly reminded her youngest, even though his brother was in another state, they were still a family and he could call his big brother any time he wanted. That little bit of reassurance can mean the world, not only to the child at home, but to your oldest who has been thrown into an entirely different world of his/her own.

One way to integrate both worlds for your kids is to make sure the younger sibling is able to visit his college-aged brother or sister at school. Most universities highly suggest (some even have a written policy) that college freshmen not have visitors for the first two weeks or even the first month of school. The rationale is based on an impressive body of research which shows the best ways for college freshmen to make a successful transition from home to school. However, once this moratorium is lifted, or during your first visit to see your collegian, make sure to take younger siblings along.

Have them sleep in the dorm and eat in the dining hall to get a real glimpse into college life; or even sit in on a class. Not only will your younger child benefit, but it will be a great way to reinforce the familial relationship to your college student.

For Laurel, mother of two boys and a girl, when her sons left for college three years apart, she recalls they both exhibited so much independence during their senior year of high school that they were more than ready to move out. "They were both chomping at the bit to be on their own and prove that they were men," she recalls. So much so that when they came home for Thanksgiving their first year, they weren't expecting a curfew because they had changed so much, but as Laurel puts it, "I hadn't changed." With a younger daughter still at home, she was still used to curfews and having her high schooler come in and tell her when she was home safely. Which meant that Laurel had trouble sleeping when the boys would come home at various times of the night over college breaks. Eventually they figured out a new system together; when the last one came home he would turn off the light in the hall. That way, if Laurel woke up in the middle of the night worried whether they were all home safely, she'd notice the hall light had been turned off and could go peacefully back to sleep.

Another thing Laurel and her kids still at home learned after the eldest went off to college was that kids don't automatically absorb the things adults take for granted. This became a great lesson to her younger kids, who went to college without assuming they knew everything they needed to know, and learned a lot from their older brother, both from his successes and mistakes.

It's OK to Be Excited

When the time comes for your last child to leave home, making you a true empty nester, you may feel grief, panic, relief, freedom, or even excitement. It all depends on you, the family dynamic, and your relationship with each of your children individually. If you're looking forward to this next chapter in your life and marriage, that's perfectly healthy. And it is also a blessing. Embrace this feeling of anticipation and don't feel guilty about it. Allow yourself to enjoy and revel in your newfound independence. And time!

Both Laurel and Jeanne had their last child leave home the same year, and since the families were close – all three kids about the same age – it was reassuring for both mothers to become empty nesters at the same time. "We were excited and nervous," recalls Laurel. "We processed a lot together, trying to figure out – who are we now? We knew God had something else planned for each of us, but didn't know what it was going to be. I felt pressure to figure it out for myself, but learned that I had to have the patience for him to bring it about in his time."

Jeanne admits, "I think I'm not like a lot of other moms since I was really excited for my kids that they were all launching in good, healthy ways. I looked forward to my husband and myself being empty nesters since we had such a blessed marriage."

CHAPTER SEVEN

Visiting Your College Student – What to Expect

Chances are, before you've survived move-in and the dreaded goodbyes mentioned in detail in Chapter Four, you have probably already made plans, in your own mind, about when you will visit your college student. Here's a tip: even if you aren't a planner, get something on the calendar before your student leaves home. "The thing that helps me the most is knowing when our next visit is – even if it's three months away," says Kristen. "There is nothing greater than when you get to see them and be a little part of their life at college."

Just as important, make sure to ask your student when he/she wants you to visit, so you both have the same plan. Otherwise, showing up at their dorm three weeks before Parents Weekend may not necessarily be a welcome surprise, while skipping it entirely could be a big bummer if your child was expecting to introduce you to their new friends' parents. Again, let your child be your guide. They will tell you when their preferred visit time is, and it will give you both something to look forward to so you're not wondering about when you will physically see each other next.

The Big Kahuna: Campus Visit #1

As luck would have it, Parents Weekend for both of our twins' schools happened to fall on the exact same weekend. Our daughter was all about it and couldn't wait to show off her campus, friends, favorite restaurants, stores, and routine. Me? I panicked. My husband and I would have to split up, just like we had done for swim meets and dance competitions for the last decade. How can a mother even try to pick which of her twins she wants to see on a college Parents Weekend? The need to see *both* my son and daughter in their respective environments was overwhelming. Then and only then would I truly know how happy or unhappy they were, how much they missed me, if they were homesick, how their appearance had changed to look older, wiser, more mature. Just as my husband was about to have to peel me off the ceiling due to my angst, our son's swim coaches let us know most freshmen parents opted out of Parents Weekend, so they could come to a big swim meet that hosted 10 other teams in November instead. Crisis averted!

I'll never forget the first visit to see our daughter, on Parents Weekend, which also happened to fall on my birthday. Armed with great advice from other empty nesters, I did my best to keep my expectations in check, reminding myself she would have dance rehearsals, studying, and other activities going on that weekend, so we wouldn't have her all to ourselves. My husband and I packed gym clothes, planning to work out at the Student Rec Center, while our daughter was busy with other things, and we also bought our own football tickets, knowing she would rather sit in student seating than with us fuddy-duddys much farther up in the stands. I carefully planned what to wear to impress her new friends as the "cool" mom and constantly checked my expectations at the door. Still, I was nervous.

Then, a few days before we were about to leave, our daughter Snapchated me a photo of her, my husband, and myself from one of her many high school dance concerts with her in the middle of us enveloped in hugs and proud smiles. Underneath was a ticker that said, "2 days, 17 hours, 54 minutes, and 17 seconds until Parents Weekend!" In that singular moment, my nerves calmed and the only thing that mattered was that, in just a few short days, I was going to see my baby girl.

The weekend itself? Better than expected. Our daughter graciously spent far more time with us than we thought possible, made my birthday extra special by ordering my favorite cake from a local bakery, and gave me a gift certificate to a store she deemed "the Fort Collins version" of my favorite store at home – then took me shopping there! Come Sunday night, after we had pizza in our hotel room, and when we knew we had to get up early to catch a flight the next morning, my husband had to physically extract her from our room to drive her back to her dorm. I cried myself to sleep, having forgotten that seeing her meant saying goodbye. All over again. And boy, did it hurt.

Campus Visit #2: A Month Later

Having survived the roller coaster of emotions after visiting our daughter for the first time, a month later it was our turn to finally see our son. We followed the same protocol, trying not to expect too much, but the bar had already been set. Did this even occur to me as our flight touched down after five long hours and we anticipated seeing our son for the first time in two-and-a-half months? Not a chance. All I wanted was to give him a big hug, hold him in my arms, and spend every moment he wasn't swimming with him. Ah, but such is not the way that prelims/finals swim meets work.

The night before the meet was just perfect – reuniting with our son at our hotel and having a Polaroid moment before meeting his new best friend/teammate and his friend's parents for an Italian dinner. Carbs and protein, every swimmer's best friend. While the place wasn't fancy and the wine was just shy of being drinkable, I luxuriated in getting to know his friend and seeing the easy camaraderie between both of them. We loved hearing the stories about the team and it really sounded like the coaches had done a great job of creating a family atmosphere for the boys. The upperclassmen looked out for the underclassmen, and the kids all took care of each other and cheered each other on through nine swims and three lifts a week, including morning practices that had them waking up at 5:30 a.m.

The following three days were a blur. Since prelims were in the mornings, we'd watch our son swim, and then had just enough time to take him out for a quick lunch before he went back to his dorm room and napped, arriving back at the pool just prior to warming up to swim finals. The Athletic Department provided the swimmers with packaged dinners every night, which they took back to their dorms or ate at the pool so they could get to sleep as soon as possible and recover for the next day of swimming. Definitely not part of my plan.

We made the best of the extra time, sightseeing and shopping, and pretending to enjoy dinners all to ourselves. But I was disappointed. And frustrated that we had flown all that way to see him for just a few short hours each day. Although in hindsight, it made perfect sense. Our son was, after all, a Division 1 swimmer, fighting it out against the real thing, each and every day of the three-day meet. By the time our flight left the following Monday he was exhausted, starting to get sick, and already behind in classes. And yes, I cried myself to sleep before we left.

Subsequent Visits: The Band-Aid Gets Ripped Off

The good news is, no matter what your first campus visit experience with your child is like, they only get better from there. As time passes, your kids miss you more and as they begin to mature and grow they realize just how much you, as a parent, have done and continue to do for them. And even though every time you see them during their first year in college you have to say goodbye again, each time it hurts a little less and you recover a little faster. The key is to manage expectations (like I did during our first college visit, but not during our second!), let your child take the lead on how often/when/where to see you, and to make as much of your time together as possible. Get to know their friends, really get to know them – ask about their career plans, where they're from, and fully embrace the memories they've already shared with your son or daughter. Show them a glimpse into your family with photos of siblings, funny stories of your child growing up, or inside family jokes to bridge the gap between college life and home life. This way, when you talk on the phone with your student, you can ask how so-and-so is doing and be able to visualize that person and ask specific questions about their interests.

It's also important to put each visit in perspective and know that every campus visit doesn't have to be like the one before. When we visited our son for the final swim meet of his freshman season, even though we still only saw him for meals, this time we were expecting it and were grateful for the limited amount of time we had. We were also armed with a list of other things to do, on our own, while we were in the city. And my interactions with him got better with each and every visit, because I knew his friends, was interested in his new life, and showed him as much by how we related to each other. The benefits of this connection with his college life are not just tenfold, but a thousandfold.

Not only did our son thank me every day for coming during our second visit, but he also gave me more hugs, let my hugs linger longer, and was truly fascinated when I told him about writing this book. He was encouraging and, dare I say, even a bit impressed given that I'd gone from a website editor to "retired," just a week before he graduated, to full-time author. Best of all, he promised to be home in time for Mother's Day, and was genuinely empathetic at my now-standard cry fest during our goodbyes, instead of being annoyed like he had been when he was a sophomore in high school going to camp for two weeks. Two weeks – what was I thinking back then?

Unlike some other parents, we gave both kids the choice of whether or not to come home for Spring Break during their freshman year. One elected to spend it somewhere else with their new friends, while the other popped in for a few days. Was I disappointed they both didn't come home for a full week? A little, but not really shocked. It was just another sign they were growing up, becoming independent, and right where they were supposed to be.

If You Can't Visit

Even though my husband and I were blessed with the ability to visit our kids once a semester, I know that simply isn't realistic for many families. Especially with the cost of college education these days and so many kids going out of state, or even across the country. Instead of feeling guilty or sad, turn your potentially negative energy into something positive by spending a few weeks thoughtfully collecting items for a care package for your student. I've learned from experience that if you have a specific list of obscure goodies, it will only add to your stress, but if you keep your eyes open to things that would bring a smile to your college student's face, or stomach, you'll be amazed at what just jumps into your cart at the grocery store or Target. T.J. Maxx is one of my favorite places to find goodies for care packages since they have everything from shampoo and shower gel to candy to frames to T-shirts and socks, all at great prices.

You can pick a theme – a holiday, place you've recently visited, or mix it up, and fill a small, recycled shipping box with things that will remind your son or daughter of home, family, or their favorite snacks. If you have time, wrap each item in inexpensive tissue paper, or recycled newspaper, which will give your student more to unwrap and allow them to be surprised by each item. I've only done this a few times, but each time I do, my daughter loves it. For Easter, I wrapped everything in pastel colors, and didn't even tape the tissue paper. She said it looked like her desk "had a little party" when she finished unwrapping all of her goodies.

And don't forget the first time your student gets sick, like with a bad cold, or heaven forbid, the flu. It's easy to use Amazon to create your own care package of Ramen noodles, tea bags, warm socks, Vitamin C gummies, or cough drops to make mom, dad, and home seem a little less far away.

CHAPTER EIGHT

Your New Role – Coaching vs. Managing

When you send your child off to college, there is a sense of accomplishment, a sense of loss, and the unrealistic expectation that your job as a parent is complete. This is partially true in the short term since cooking, cleaning, laundry, chauffeuring, and disciplining as you knew it are essentially over. Remember the good old days when "time outs: were the end-all solution for any bad behavior? Don't forget, you still have the ability to be a parent to your adult children and they still need you. Even though, at first, they may act like they don't.

Parenting adult children is a totally different dynamic, and honestly, one I personally enjoy much more than the previous stages. Not that everyone would agree, but parenting adult children can be far more rewarding than endlessly feeding bottles and changing 36 diapers a day. (If that number seems inflated, it's a twin thing — everything is doubled. Even the amount of spit up.)

My friend Kristen offered this nugget of wisdom about how to parent young adults: "Your role on the other end of the phone is being their coach when your kids are in college." This made me curious, and admittedly a bit anxious, to see what coaching looked like and how it felt. Surprisingly, my chance to experience it firsthand happened just a few weeks after my daughter was away at school. Classes had started and the fun of Welcome Week had faded to a distant memory. She was adjusting to her course load, easily finding where her classes were located, and enjoying the myriad of dining options on campus. She had also made lots of different friends — there were the girls in her dorm; kids in the dance program; she had joined the Navigators, a Christian-based college organization; and was part of a Bible study. So when she called on a random day of the week without much to say, my mother's instinct kicked in that something was up. Still, I played it cool and waited for her to be the one to let me in on the reason for her impromptu phone call.

Apparently she had been to a fraternity party, didn't like it, and as a result was questioning her decision to go through recruitment to join a sorority, which was scheduled to start the following week. Keep in mind this is the girl who eliminated potential colleges if they didn't have a thriving Greek system, in addition to other factors, of course. My daughter had decided while we were on one of our eight college visits that sorority life was for her. When I suggested we start visiting sorority houses on the various campuses we toured, this sealed the deal. For her, Greek life was about the sisterhood, activities, and DIY projects (a forte of hers long before Pinterest ever existed). Plus, she thought the whole big/little sister thing was adorable.

Once it became clear she was calling for advice, I was careful to give her insights into the decision without telling her exactly what to do. I told her sororities were only about fraternity parties if you wanted that to be your focus, and reminded her of all the other reasons she had been interested in becoming part of Greek life. Then I explained how the recruitment process worked, suggesting she just go for the first day and, if she didn't like it, then she didn't have to continue. Or, if she got to the end of the process and decided not to pledge a sorority, then at least she would have had the choice. She thanked me profusely and hung up telling me she'd let me know what she decided in a few days.

Sitting on my patio chair in the sun, holding the phone in my hand after our call, two realizations occurred to me. First, my daughter still needed me (praise God!) and second, it was crystal clear what my new role was as a parent. No longer was I managing her day-to-day life. Instead, she now sought advice from me when she needed it, so I was gently coaching her along the journey. A wave of gratitude swept over me.

What Does Coaching Look Like?

According to Laurel, coaching means, "Letting your kids make more decisions on their own and learning the consequences of those decisions, which is still a hard thing for a parent to do." She strongly believes that talking things out with your adult children is important, although she admits that both she and her husband probably over-explained things sometimes, which was just part of the learning process. With all three of her children out of college, married, and some having children of their own now, Laurel wisely advises, "It is best to wait to be asked for your input and then parcel it out in little pieces."

Part of coaching versus managing means lightening up on rules and expectations. This, combined with the time apart, helps you more easily step back and be less parental than you've been in the past. Cindy recalls when her relationship with her oldest child changed. It was after her daughter had attended college for a year and a half, and then embarked on a three-month mission trip to Peru. "We began moving out of the parent/child relationship and were becoming more like peers," says Cindy. "When she was home, we definitely didn't have any expectations of her like when she was in high school; we didn't have curfews, and just tried to spend time with her. We hoped she would come to us for counsel, which she did, and we had more adult conversations with her."

Therein lies the benefit of becoming a little less parental and more of a coach. You can thrive in adult relationships with your kids, in ways you never thought possible, and all of your lives will be richer for it.

Support When You're Not There

Since you aren't managing your college student's everyday life anymore, there will be times when he or she needs some other adult support. If you live some distance away from their school, this compounds the fact that you simply can't be there instantly in the case of an emergency. Having someone who knows your child and lives in or close to the town where your student attends school can be a blessing. It could be a coach, someone in the counseling office, an RA, or even a friend of the family. "Making little personal connections always makes me feel better," says Kristen, whose eldest son's lacrosse coach went to his dorm room and took him to the doctor after he got a concussion.

Similarly, Kristen's younger son went to a college where their neighbor and childhood babysitter now actually worked in the counseling office on campus. This former neighbor would invite him over for dinner or to bake bread and hang out, giving him a little break from campus life and a taste of home. Kristen said, "Just knowing we could call her at any time if something happened, and she could step in before we could get there, really helped our comfort level."

In my family's case, we were lucky enough to have my husband's aunt in the city where our son attended school. Due to his intense swim schedule, he really didn't see her his freshman year. Despite Aunt Patty's willingness to have him out to the suburbs for dinner – her community was not an easy destination to get to for a college kid without transportation. Still, we knew that should something happen, we had family close by who could be there before we could catch a five-hour flight. Additionally, Aunt Patty's daughter was a lawyer who was also married to a lawyer. Both of them gently reminded us that, should our son be in need of an attorney (not that such a thing would ever happen) she and her husband could be there on the spot since they lived in the city.

When our daughter moved away to school, a seven-and-a-half-hour drive or short one-hour flight, we thought we didn't have any connections in her town. Over the course of her first year of college, though, I reconnected with an old friend who happened to live just 45 minutes away from campus. She came up for our daughter's fall and spring dance concerts, which meant the world to our dancer, and while the girls didn't spend more than a few minutes talking to each other after the shows, it put our mind at ease that Mary could drive to campus sooner than we could. She would even let me know when she was in town teaching yoga classes in case our daughter needed anything.

If you don't have similar connections, not to worry. Chances are your student will seek out mentors at school who can help in the same way as family or friends. And remember to pay it forward when you have friends' kids attending college close to where you live. I happily invited twin freshmen, who had been friends with my kids since kindergarten, over for dinner and took them out to lunch, when they attended school just an hour away from our home.

Summer After Freshman Year: You Want to Do What?

It never occurred to me that neither of my kids would be home for the summer between their freshman and sophomore years of college. I knew, of course, this summer would be different than the last, given their newfound independence and our need to respect that freedom by not enforcing curfews or a whole bunch of rules. Both kids' finals schedules ensured they would be home for Mother's Day (my favorite holiday, other than Christmas). Let's face it, moms do a lot of work to make Christmas happen and on Mother's Day we don't have to do anything other than spend the whole day with our families! In my mind, that translated to roughly three months when both kids would be living under the same roof.

So when my daughter pulled me aside during Christmas Break of her freshman year and said, "Mom, don't take this personally, but three months is a long time to be at home for the summer," my heart sank as my vision of the last summer with both kids at home appeared to be circling the drain. My ambitious young marine biology/zoology major then proceeded to lay out all the options she had already researched for summer jobs, internships, and study abroad programs. They ranged from spending the whole summer working in the state where she attended school (really, the entire summer?) to studying abroad in Mexico (was that safe?) or Honduras (which seemed even less safe than Mexico) to getting an internship in Australia (on the other side of the world!). While I tried to remain calm and keep it together since this was her decision and not mine, I realized this was going to be an even bigger coaching moment than when she called for advice about whether or not to join a sorority.

Before you assume my reaction was as calm as a glacial lake, let me assure you that was far from reality. Instead, I dropped my daughter off at home and then drove to a quiet, secluded place and erupted into gut-wrenching sobs which left me drained and confused.

Over the next few months, I listened and provided advice, only when asked, as my daughter sorted through her options, finally settling on the study abroad internship in Australia. Truth be told, as she was eliminating each of the other possibilities, I knew in my heart the Australia option was the perfect way to set herself up for a virtually unlimited number of internship options back in the States during subsequent summers. After all, once she'd interned for a marine biology program in Sydney, Australia, any aquarium in the U.S. would be thrilled to have her. Given that working with marine mammals had been a dream of hers since she was in the sixth grade, who was I to get in the way? Plus, the internship was only eight weeks long, so she would be home for the week after Mother's Day and then home for a month before she headed back to school.

After she'd made her decision, we were having dinner with friends who had a junior in high school, twin high school freshmen, and a son in middle school. When we told them about our daughter's plans for the summer, my friend reacted with a tinge of horror and said, "Well, just don't let her go!" I chuckled and explained it really didn't work like that when your kids were adults, and despite my preference to have her home for the summer, this was an opportunity of a lifetime. As I heard myself talking, it was a bit of an out-of-body experience.

Two years earlier, when my daughter had been a junior in high school, I would have probably reacted exactly the same way as my friend did, but here I was not only accepting the fact, but encouraging her to travel halfway across the world, all by herself.

When we shared these plans with her twin brother, his reaction was the opposite of my friend's. He paused for a moment, taking it all in, and then looked at me and said, "Well, you can't not let her go." To which I replied, with a knowing smile, that not only wasn't I "not letting her go," but we were actually paying for the experience. He was quiet for another minute and then said, "I mean, I'm going to miss her and everything, but I guess my summer is going to be a little different now." He clearly had been anticipating his sister's return as well. Especially since he was planning on this being his last summer at home to train with his club swim team, and spend as much time backpacking with his friends as possible in between working a summer job.

Unfortunately for our daughter, the story doesn't end there. The first day of final exams of spring semester of her freshman year, during which she had to take no less than three tests in a single day, our potential marine biologist found out the nonprofit organization responsible for internship placements in Sydney "didn't have any opportunities for her to work directly with marine animals." The Vice President of International Studies at our daughter's college, who had been working directly with the nonprofit, was furious and flatly refused their suggestion that our daughter fly to the other side of the world to work in an administrative position. She also informed the nonprofit they would be reimbursing us for a very expensive plane ticket. Sadly, the same thing happened to our daughter's friend, who had also been accepted into the program, proving the nonprofit, who shall remain nameless for purposes of this book, was in over their head and had let a number of students down, just a week before they were to fly to Australia. Gut-wrenching.

Bracing for our daughter's reaction, my husband and I were both shocked at how well she handled this extremely unfair situation. After a few minutes of tears, she got angry, and rightfully so, demanding the name and phone number of the university's contact at the nonprofit. Our girl had every intention of giving them a piece of her mind. We agreed this was a good idea since the nonprofit should be held accountable for their actions. Then we started brainstorming other ideas for her to work at an aquarium in the U.S., even though most internships had likely been given out months before. She said she'd think about it and went off to successfully complete her remaining exams for the day. Unbeknownst to us, when she should have been studying for her last and most difficult exam, which was Chemistry (need I say more), she began researching any other possible study abroad options that still had openings. Keep in mind this was mid-May and most international programs start June 1.

Imagine our surprise when the phone rang at 11 p.m. that same night and our strong-willed, tenacious zoology major informed us she had found a study abroad opportunity with one single opening, and had completed half of the application online. After she explained the details, we wholeheartedly encouraged her to pursue it and suggested, via coaching, that she set up a conference call with the Vice President of International

Studies at her school to see if she could help make this dream a reality. Fully expecting our daughter would meet with the V.P. alone, we were thrilled when she called us the next morning, while we were en route to pick her up from school, and asked us to be part of the conference call.

In a whirlwind of activity, our daughter submitted her completed application, including transcripts, letters of recommendation, and various other documents that sent her traversing campus numerous times in less than 24 hours. At the same time, the V.P. of International Studies secured an interview for her with the woman in charge of selecting the final student for the study abroad program.

While my husband and I moved all of her belongings out of her dorm room, our daughter was camped out in her beanbag, the only remaining piece of furniture that was hers, answering questions that would determine her fate that summer. Forty minutes later, as I was walking into her room for the final load, my daughter informed me that she was the last student accepted into a Turks and Caicos study abroad program! My heart soared with pride, relief, and excitement for her, before I even knew how long the program would be. Huh, seems like we both learned a lot from that experience.

Lest you think the Turks and Caicos experience was a resort-like study abroad, keep in mind the program took place in South Caicos, a tiny island still rebuilding from a massive hurricane, where freshwater was so scarce that the students washed their clothes in saltwater and were only allowed one freshwater shower a week. The entire facility was open air, meaning it was hot and humid with flies taking up permanent residence in the outside dining hall. There was no air conditioning in the rooms where the students stayed at night, so my daughter slept with a fan at her head and one at her feet for a month. She attended four lectures a day, read voraciously, wrote papers, took tests identifying various fish, and completed a final exam. But...she snorkeled at least twice a week, researching the ocean water and its marine life, and sharing with the South Caicos community what she and her classmates had learned about this precious resource. It was the experience of a lifetime.

When I shared with Laurel the kids' summer plans, our daughter studying abroad, and our son planning on making this his last summer at home, she empathized with me and the feeling that they were both getting just a little farther away from the mother ship. "We were very philosophical about it when it happened to us, because we knew it was coming, but it was another step," she said. "It was hard, but felt like the natural progression of things."

CHAPTER NINE

First Visit Home – It Will Be Different

For some families whose children go to school out of state, it just isn't feasible to visit your college student before the November/December holidays. Especially with schools on the trimester system that don't start until the end of September. Whether the logistics of your child's chosen place of higher learning requires the use of planes, trains, or automobiles, for you to get there or them to get home, chances are you may not have the option of visiting your child on campus. Which means it's a very real possibility that the first time you'll see them, after dropping them off at college, is during a holiday break based solely on their school schedule. Be forewarned, their time at home may not be exactly as you had planned and it certainly won't be "just like" previous holidays.

The fact is, your child has become more independent while living on his/her own for the last few months, and that's a good thing. But it also means expecting this holiday to be like the 17 or 18 preceding it, just isn't realistic. Your college student is still making the transition from living under your guidance to living on his/her own in a whole new environment. While some may thrive in those first few months, others may struggle. No two kids are the same and boys tend to be a bit different than girls.

When Your Child Is Ready To Come Home

In an ideal world, your college student would be excited to come home for the holidays and maybe even have a countdown timer like our daughter did for Parents Weekend. If it makes you feel any better, we didn't get a countdown calendar for Thanksgiving break, even though our daughter was indeed ready to come home. As the week approached, our phone conversations revolved around how excited she was to sleep in her comfy double bed, which would feel enormous compared to the skinny twin, extra-long mattress she had been slumbering on for the last three months. She talked about how much she missed our dog and couldn't wait to hold our fuzzy, soft, poodle/bichon mix in her arms and snuffle his fur. She reminisced about which friends she was hoping to see and which dance classes she was going to take at her "old" dance studio. Never once did she talk about how much she missed us, which in hindsight made perfect sense, since we had visited her just a month before.

Despite our attempts at offering unsolicited advice to the contrary, our daughter was planning to work every day she was home, since her summer job had been in retail and we all know how Black Friday has spread into Thanksgiving Day and the subsequent weekend. Really? It is a national holiday, after all, but that's a whole other book on American culture.

Given all of this prelude, you would think my expectations would have been lowered about how often we would see our daughter. Not a chance. Visions of family dinners together every night, followed by our precollege ritual of watching a show that all four of us enjoyed on Netflix, still danced through my head. Once the optimist, always the optimist. We knew of course, that she would spend time with her high school friends – those who were still underclassmen and those who had gone to college and were home for the holiday. But I continued to hold out hope for Norman Rockwell family moments, just the four of us.

The reality is, we saw her for a limited amount of time each day, in between all of her previously mentioned commitments, and ended up being disappointed with how little time we spent together as a family. Had I learned nothing from visiting both of my kids at college? Of course. I just didn't have the foresight to apply it to when they visited us at home.

It took until after the weekend was over for me to realize that any time we spent with her was a gift. And quite frankly, to have both of my kids sleeping in their own rooms above me and coming and going at various times of the day made our home come alive again. And that was surely something to be thankful for.

When Your Child Would Rather Be at School

On the other end of the spectrum is the student who doesn't think he'll want to come home for a school break because he is truly expressing his independence. Laurel's eldest child was so set on approaching everything about college on his own that he didn't even let his parents help him move in. He simply had them drop him at the airport with a whole bunch of duffel bags and he was off. Not surprisingly, this same kid insisted he didn't want to come home for Thanksgiving. However, Laurel and her husband wisely bought him a ticket and didn't tell him, just in case he changed his mind. Which he did. Thankfully, his parents already had an airline ticket in hand, without the last minute price increases, something especially crucial since he was flying home from the other side of the country.

Then there are the students who simply aren't ready to come home for a school break, because they are having too much fun with their new friends, new life, and newfound independence. This was exactly the case when our son came home for Thanksgiving. We had just seen him on campus the weekend before, but did that occur to me as we drove to the airport to pick him up? Not a chance. My boy was coming home and I was going to love on him by cooking his favorite meals and relishing his presence. Numerous Costco, grocery, and Target stops the week before ensured that all of his favorite foods were stocked in the pantry, and I even baked homemade banana chocolate chip bread, both of my kids' favorite, in advance of their visits.

So you can imagine my dismay when, as we were driving home from the airport, I asked which high school friends he was most looking forward to seeing, and his immediate, honest answer was, "I really don't know. I just already miss all of my friends at school." Such a sentiment should have given me insight into where his head was at, but instead I attributed it to the fact that he was exhausted, since he and his teammates had gone out the night before they all flew home. When asked if he was excited to sleep in his own bed, he simply replied that his bed at school was perfectly fine. Really, a twin extra-long mattress was comfortable for a swimmer over six feet tall whose wingspan measured six feet four inches? Not to mention the fact that this was a guy who still, beyond my understanding, somehow managed to sleep perpendicular in his bed for part of the night, just like when he was a toddler. In hindsight, it is easy to see the positive side of his attachment to college life. He was happy. He felt settled. He treasured his new friendships and best of all, or worst, depending on his mama's view of the world, he considered college his new home.

The next few days were painful for me, as it became clear he simply didn't want to be home. While he was cordial with his grandparents and aunt during Thanksgiving dinner, the rest of the time he was grumpy and withdrawn. I bemoaned to my husband that I had "lost him" and snuck into my bedroom and broke down in tears more than once.

We tried the old style of parenting, which worked when both kids lived under our roof – calling him out on his attitude and telling him that he at least had to be cordial to the rest of us. While this strategy helped a little, it was clear he still wanted to be somewhere else, and that wasn't at home. I was baffled, hurt, and confused.

Then, the day before he was supposed to fly back to school, it all became crystal clear. My husband and I took him out to breakfast, since food is his love language, while his sister was at work, so it was just the three of us. We let him choose the place and since it was a favorite local spot, one of his friends from high school, who was also swimming in college, just happened to be there. She came up to our table, visited awhile, and mentioned that she wasn't ready to go back to school yet, even though she had been home for a full week, instead of just a few days like our son. When she asked if he was ready to go back, he answered with a huge smile and an unequivocal, "Yes!" His friend looked at my husband and me in a kind way and said, "That's good, right? That's really good!" While I was still processing that an 18-year-old girl had figured out how lucky I was to have a kid who not only liked his college choice, but actually loved it and was ready for Thanksgiving break to end, my son put the final piece of the puzzle together. He told his friend, "Well, I just saw my parents a few days before I came home since they came out to see me swim." Cue a huge lightbulb flashing over my head and my husband looking at me with a sweet, I-told-you-so look confirming it was all about our son and had nothing to do with me or my prowess as a mom.

As if that wasn't enough reassurance, my daughter called after she was safely back at school and told me that she and her brother had a great conversation in the airport while they were both waiting to board their flights. Even though they were flying on separate airlines, they were boarding at gates directly next to each other, which is when it became crystal clear that it was God's plan for them to have this gift of time to talk. Just the two of them.

My daughter also told me that she had sensed the tension between me and my son over the break, and that she had talked to him about it. He told her he was just missing school and his new friends, and that it was no reflection on how he felt about me or my husband, or even being back home for the first time in 12 weeks. Then, to my amazement, she gently gave me some unsolicited advice that made me realize how much she had matured in just the last few months. She said, "Mom, you shouldn't take it personally. He's a boy and has a different way of communicating than you and I do, but it doesn't mean he loves you any less." In that moment, my heart was finally at peace as it became clear that I hadn't "lost" my son at all. He was growing up and pulling away from the nest, just as he should be. And so was my daughter, but in a slightly different way. It was like their childhood home was a space station and they were each doing a spacewalk at their own pace – still attached to home via a cord that kept them from floating aimlessly in space, but one that kept getting a little bit longer and farther away as they became more and more independent – sometimes in baby steps and other times in giant leaps.

The kicker of this somewhat drama-filled holiday was when, a few weeks afterward, my husband was having coffee with his former business partners, both of whom were empty nesters well before us. As they were catching up on their respective jobs and families, they both asked my husband how our Thanksgiving visit had been with our kids. When he told them what had happened, they both nodded sagely and said, "Oh yeah. Our kids' first visit at home totally sucked." When my husband relayed the story to me, we both looked at each other and said aloud, "Why didn't anybody tell us this stuff?" And that was just one more impetus for this book – to help prepare future empty nesters from getting blindsided by stuff like this.

CHAPTER TEN

First Holiday Apart – You Will Survive

We were lucky in the sense that the first holiday we spent home without both of our kids was Easter, a full seven months after we dropped them off at college. Since many of their friends weren't even able to make it home for Thanksgiving, we realized how blessed we were to not have to experience a holiday, sans kids, until the spring of their freshman year. So you think it would be no big deal, right? I tried to convince myself of this fact while assembling the Easter egg tree centerpiece and putting out the rest of the decorations, including adorable bunny bowls, without my kids there to see them. Who would sneak jelly beans out of the glass eggs that resided on the windowsill every spring? On a side note, I didn't decorate for Halloween, knowing they wouldn't be home then either, but since they hadn't gone trick or treating in years, that seemed like a slightly less emotional holiday anyway.

So why did Easter feel like such a big deal without my son and daughter at home? It wasn't until a week before the actual holiday that the solution occurred to me. This would be the first time in 18 years we wouldn't do an Easter egg hunt at our house or have the kids search for their baskets. Never mind that I had carefully selected their favorite goodies and sent each of them an Easter care package at school. It still wasn't the same as them waking up to mini chocolate eggs scattered throughout the house, just like my parents had done for me.

When I was a little girl there were only the traditional, foil-wrapped Hershey mini chocolate eggs, which my parents deemed much easier to hide than real eggs or plastic ones filled with toys or money. So when the twins were born we continued the tradition of hiding chocolate eggs as soon as they were toddlers. Over the years as candy manufacturers got more and more creative, we hid Nestle Crunch chocolate eggs one year and Reese's peanut butter eggs another. During our kids' senior year of high school when I couldn't find the highly sought-after miniature Reese's eggs, it caused great disappointment throughout our household, even though I'd managed to snag a bag of Nestle Crunch ones instead. A few days later, while shopping with my daughter, we found the coveted Reese's mini eggs and ended up with double the number of chocolate eggs that year. On the cusp of adulthood, my kids were thrilled to search for a total of 50 pastel-colored, hidden, mouthwatering delights.

This tradition, combined with all of us attending Easter service together, in the same row of the same church that we had attended ever since they were five years old, made me get choked up the Sunday before Easter as our pastor described the events for Holy Week, including the three different Easter Sunday services. I actually teared up imagining what it would be like without my son and daughter sitting next to us. Even my mom, who had moved to our town four years earlier, wouldn't be at church with us on Easter since she was on a cruise halfway around the world – quite impressive for an 82-year-old woman to travel alone for two months. But in my state of self-pity, all I could think was that our Easter traditions were crushed and nothing could make it better.

Create New Traditions as a Couple

Throughout this rather melodramatic period, which I chose to blame on menopause and fluctuating hormones, my dear husband had the brilliant idea to start a new tradition as a couple on Easter. Instead of coming home from church to an empty house, he suggested we go out to brunch afterwards. If there is one meal I am partial to, it's a traditional brunch buffet with lots of different types of food – from Eggs Benedict to bacon and French toast to pancakes. Not to mention pastries galore, which often come in bite-sized portions making it seem less sinful to eat three, four, or even five. I feel compelled to try each kind, since the pastry chef put all that time and energy into making them!

Brunch turned out to be a fun date, followed by an Easter egg hunt with our dog, a poodle/bichon mix. Thankfully, our daughter had started this tradition a few years prior when she filled plastic eggs with pieces of kibble and hid them in the living room while our dog patiently waited in the bathroom. We continued the tradition after Easter brunch which resulted in a white fluff ball charging out of the bathroom in search of plastic eggs. He then proceeded to break them open with his mouth to get to the kibble inside before furiously traversing the living room in search of more treasures. Nothing can make you smile the way a dog can, let alone one hell-bent on finding extra pieces of kibble. We even FaceTimed both kids to show them the doggie egg hunt, so we could all enjoy Cooper's joy together.

Serve Others

In addition to our new couple's tradition, we decided to invite our neighbor to church with us. She typically attended a Catholic mass on Easter, but had been saying for weeks that she wanted to join us at our church, so we invited her along. She had been going through some challenges of her own, and she was so grateful for the company and the change in her routine.

After showing her the kids' wing of the church, the teen/youth group "loft," and handing her a steaming hot cup of coffee from the free coffee station, I noticed that her whole demeanor changed. It was clear that she felt lighter and happier simply being there. She even remarked, "This is what church should be like," with a lobby filled with kids and parents, a rocking praise band, and packed worship sanctuary.

Handing her a tissue to dry her tears during the course of the service, I suddenly realized how wonderful it felt to be loving on her and making her feel welcome in a new place of worship. We introduced her to our friends after church and she went back home to spend the day with her young son, while we went to our new tradition of Easter brunch. The irony was that she kept thanking *us* for bringing *her,* while I felt truly blessed to have her there to nurture and strengthen, just as I would have with my own kids.

Encourage Your Kids to Create New Traditions

Since it wasn't feasible to fly both of our kids home for Easter, and they preferred to stay at school anyway to prepare for the end of the semester with final exams looming in the near future, we encouraged them to make Easter plans at their respective schools. Our son attended his first-ever Catholic mass with his best friend, who went nearly every Sunday. When I asked which church they were attending, a few days before Easter, my son said he had told his friend to "pick his favorite." They ended up at a beautiful chapel, right in the middle of campus, with a statue dedicated to Martin Luther King Jr. adorning the plaza outside.

Our daughter had several offers from her friends' families, with whom she had spent time over Spring Break, to join them for Easter weekend at their respective homes. Instead, she elected to stay at school, having just completed a four-day dance competition that resulted in her missing two days of classes. While I was hesitant that staying on campus would feel like living in a ghost town, she assured me that a bunch of her friends were doing the same thing, since the end of the semester was just six weeks away and everyone had lots of studying to do. In an Easter experience that was the complete opposite of her brother's, she attended church at a local coffee shop known for their non-traditional Sunday services and went out to breakfast with one of her friends afterwards. One Easter, three different traditions. Somehow it felt just the way God had intended.

CHAPTER ELEVEN

Reinventing Yourself – More Than a Parent

Let's be frank. This chapter is intended for parents whose last child has left for college; empty nesters in the fullest sense of the word. Even so, let me gently suggest to anyone reading this book that you don't skip it entirely. And it's not just because I painstakingly wrote it on parchment paper by hand to make sure it was authentic, real, and emotive. Okay, I'm being a bit melodramatic. But seriously, this chapter will get you thinking ahead to how your life will change, in good and even wonderful ways, when you have no kids left at home and your life feels different at best, or off-kilter at worst.

I can now safely say, there are elements to being an empty nester that are just plain fantastic. For the first time in heaven knows how many years, your alarm clock isn't determined by someone else's schedule. If you worked outside of the home while raising your kids, chances are you still had to wake up earlier than you would have chosen to get everyone out of the house and still arrive at work on time, showered, and with a matching pair of shoes on your feet. A friend, who owned her own business, rose before the sun at 5:30 a.m. every single day that her three kids were in school, just so she could be showered and ready to hit the ground running when the rest of her pack arose a full hour later.

For my husband and me, this newfound alarm clock freedom meant the ability to leisurely sleep in until 7:30 a.m. or even later. This was a big, but welcome change from the 6 a.m. feedings when the kids were infants or worse, the 5:45 a.m. alarm clock for those lovely things called "zero hour" classes, which required our kids to arrive at their high school when it was still as dark as night. And weekends? Well, those were perfectly blissful because they didn't even require an alarm. Just imagine!

Having your house all to yourselves has advantages as well. While at the beginning it may feel like your home is too quiet, you will slowly get to the point where you realize it is just quiet enough. This allows you the gift of time, not always having to do something, so you can actually read an entire article, blog post, or chapter of a book without interruption. Or binge on Netflix without feeling guilty. Or start a project that requires concentration without the dreaded holler of "Mom!" or "Dad!" causing you to abandon where you were in the process, only to come back to it days later and have to remember how and where to start again. It will also mean you and your spouse will have the whole house to yourselves. At any time of day. Since my kids will likely read this book, I'll leave it there. I can already hear them saying, "Eeewww, did you really have to include that part, Mom?"

With the gift of time, privacy, and more sleep, many parents naturally take an inward and outward look around and think, so now what? And the answer is – you can do anything you want. Start a new career, go back to work, volunteer, start a hobby you've been wanting to try for say twenty or so years. The world is your oyster. Just like it is for your college student.

Surrogate Kids

The more you wring your hands, or heart, over all of your kids living away from home, the harder the adjustment will be. Instead, try to look for the positives. I can assure you this simple step alone will open you up to things you never imagined you were called to do.

"The best part of being an empty nester," says Laurel, "is it is a true lesson in focusing on the possibilities of what you can do now that your kids aren't at home." For she and her husband Greg, God literally flooded them with twenty-somethings to mentor. The result has been a blessing to both the couple and those they gently guide through the ups and downs of entering the real world after college and trying to find themselves. She feels like they can be friends with these young adults, who look up to them and see a marriage they want to emulate, while asking serious questions and getting real answers. "It's a huge gift and something we hadn't even anticipated. We see the value of coming alongside others at an earlier stage of life than us," reflects Laurel.

My personal experience was, essentially, panic after my kids were gone, coupled with an urgent need to fill my time since I had quit my job just a week before my twins graduated from high school. This may sound impulsive, but it was actually the result of months of decision-making. It was a part-time job, which had paid significantly less than my skills and education warranted, but one I had accepted for the flexibility while my kids were still in school. With two college orientations in my future, along with two move-ins, furnishing two dorm rooms, and attending two parents weekends, I purposely chose to resign prior to the kids' graduation in order to focus on their last summer at home and all of the aforementioned travel.

Fortunately, my therapist, an empty nester herself, suggested I take the first six months after the twins left for school to see what opportunities presented themselves. Within that span of time, it became clear that one of my callings was to be a surrogate mom to my friends' kids, when their mothers weren't available for whatever reason. Case in point, a friend had to miss her daughter's first-ever solo at a dance competition while she was traveling for business with her husband. As she was agonizing over the inability to be in two places at once, I offered to stand in for her. My daughter had done plenty of solos over the years and I'd been to more dance competitions than you could count on both hands, so I knew the drill.

The relief that swept over my friend's face was palpable, only to be outdone by the smile her daughter gave me when I arrived in her dressing room an hour before she was supposed to perform on the big day. We pinned on her headpiece using the multiple bobby pin crossover technique that I'd perfected over the years as, dare I say it, a dance mom. I watched her rehearse her solo and even walked down with her to check-in backstage. The best part came when she was waiting for the few dances before her solo to finish. She looked at me and asked, "Are you going to stay back here with me until I go on?" To which I answered, "Absolutely. While you're walking on stage, I'll just sneak out into the first row so I can watch." In that moment, this petite, beautiful dancer dressed all in white breathed a sigh of relief as her shoulders softened and she stood a little taller. Then we turned around, so we wouldn't see her competitors on stage, said a prayer, and asked God to bless her performance. Which he did, and then some.

A slightly more dramatic example of being a surrogate parent relates to the lacerated liver mentioned in the introduction to this book. One day, on my way out the door to meet someone for lunch, I noticed a friend from another state calling my cell phone and decided to return the call from the car on my way to the restaurant. Just as I was passing my husband's home office on the way to our garage, he told me that the same friend was trying to reach him as well. My mama's instinct kicked in like a force of nature, and I knew, without a doubt, that something was terribly wrong.

As I immediately returned the call, my friend, who comes from a family of seven brothers and sisters and never "loses it," was sobbing into the phone so hard that it took me a moment to realize what she was saying. Her eldest son, who was attending college just an hour away from our mountain town, had been in a ski accident and was at the emergency room, diagnosed with a lacerated liver. They were taking him by ambulance to a larger hospital in the city to determine if he needed emergency surgery. In between racking sobs of worry, his mom asked if I could go down and be with him, since she lived a plane flight away. In an instant, my lunch plans were cancelled and I drove as fast as possible, arriving at the hospital just minutes after the ambulance.

Walking into the ER, I was rewarded with a relieved smile from a young man who was like a nephew to me, even though we weren't related by blood. Best of all, he was alert and talking, so we sent a picture of him grinning to his parents, confirming that he was currently stable and in good spirits. As soon as we got an update on his status from the doctors, I promptly texted his parents and then accompanied him to the ICU, where his sister and cousins ended up joining me, each of us taking turns by his bedside until his mom arrived a few hours later. In the end, he did not need surgery, since the laceration was small enough so the liver could repair itself, which was a true blessing.

What an amazing gift to be a stand-in mom, if only for a few hours, and to have the chance to give back to a dear friend who'd been there for me, unconditionally, when one of my kids was in a terrible accident in elementary school. Weeks after the liver episode, I received a heartfelt note from the son, thanking me for "always being there for him," which brought me to tears. After all, isn't that what we all wish for our children? Other adults who can step in for us and whom we trust unequivocally, who know and love our kids almost as much as we do.

Discovering New Interests

As mentioned above, while you may feel an urgency to fill your time without kids at home, my best advice is to pause, take a breath, and recover from the milestone you just overcame. The six months I took to just "be" and rest and grieve was the best gift I could have given myself.

The same was true for Cindy, although not in the same quantifiable amount of time. As soon as her girls left the house, she started talking to her husband about things she should do and was definitely scrambling, thinking she needed to go back to work or start volunteering or embark on endless other endeavors. Her sweet husband told her, "They just graduated. We need some time to just chill." Cindy admits this was exactly the advice she needed at that point in time. "It allowed me to really go through the grieving process and not avoid what I was feeling. Otherwise, I would have gotten too busy doing other things so I wouldn't have to deal with the lonely void. My husband, in his wisdom, allowed me to have the time and space to heal," she recalls.

After some time, Cindy began to explore other interests. It started with leading a Bible study at church, then teaching the marriage class mentioned in Chapter Three, all of which led her to a new calling, which was starting one-on-one counseling. "It's just taken time for all of that to fall into place," says Cindy with a smile.

As for me, I started to explore new interests gradually, by dipping my toe in the water of a few different streams. I attempted to make a scrapbook for my daughter, something she had asked me to do for years. Since I am the least crafty or DIY person around, the project had been put off for years. So, while both kids were busy adapting to their new college lives, I gathered favorite pictures of my little girl, and even some of her own beautiful artwork, from birth to age 18, downloaded them to my computer, and used an online website to create a hardcover photobook that didn't require scrapbook paper, stickers, or cutting and pasting, except electronically and within the confines of the slick program. Sure, it may not be the same result as the beautiful handmade scrapbook my daughter had made for me years earlier that included all of the above techniques, but it was my way of completing the book as a gift to both of us.

My husband and I also decided to renew our marriage vows the summer between the kids' freshman and sophomore years of college. This was something we had been wanting to do for a while, but with the crazy summer schedules of high school students, we'd never quite found the right time. Anticipating that this might be the last summer with both twins at home, due to internships and study abroad options looming on the horizon, we all agreed on a date and I took on this slightly larger-scale project than the dreaded scrapbook, albeit with a clear end in sight.

Even though it was a small event, with roughly 20 people in attendance, I treated it like a mini wedding – picking out a dress, planning a five-course dinner after the ceremony, and selecting flowers to decorate the venues, along with bouquets for my daughter and myself and boutonnieres for my husband and son. Since it was a vow renewal, it was fun to plan without being all-consuming and void of all the accompanying stress of a full-blown wedding. It was during this process that I discovered my love for learning about and arranging fresh flowers, and started to think about setting up an apprenticeship with the florist we had selected for our vow renewal. Who knows what will come of it, but isn't that the beauty of reinventing yourself?

A New Career Is Born

Last, but certainly not least, while trying to figure out what this new chapter of my life would look like, I made the biggest decision to date. After creating an exhaustive list of all the jobs that were of no interest to me, it became crystal clear that I desperately wanted to start writing again. Throughout my varied career, I had written essays, marketing presentations, and curricula for community college courses I taught, articles for regional and national magazines, blogs, and website content. Yet despite all of this experience, writing an entire book seemed daunting. Still, it was something that had been a goal of mine since I was in high school – to become a published author. And so this book was born.

To be frank, part of the impetus was that I couldn't find any books on the market that told parents how to prepare themselves for when their kids left for college. Sure there were books about the topic in general, but they were all missing the emotive, how-to-cope piece of the journey. It became clear this was my calling when an initial stab at the Table of Contents spilled forth, with my fingers dancing uninterrupted across the keyboard of my laptop.

About halfway through the writing process, I spent a week in the town where my daughter attends college, renting a studio apartment and hunkering down to write as much or as little as I wanted with no schedule, appointments, laundry, or even cooking to distract me. In the end, it became less about filling the time between my daughter's sorority Moms Weekend and her dance concert weekend and more about the experience of writing alone. Uninterrupted, yet inspired by all of the college students around me, I wrote in my tiny flat with light streaming through the windows or in coffee shops abuzz with youth and academia, intermingled with the comforting smell of freshly brewed warm coffee.

It was through the process of writing this book that I learned what I would and wouldn't do if I had the chance to send my kids off to college for the first time again, became inspired by the women who so graciously gave of their time to share their insights, and felt compelled that others could learn from my experience as well as theirs.

CHAPTER TWELVE

IT ALL COMES AROUND AGAIN

When my son and daughter walked across that sunny football field a year and a half ago, with the wind almost blowing off their graduation caps while they accepted their diplomas, I never could have imagined writing a book about our family's preparation for college and the experience itself. If someone had predicted that I would become a published author, I probably would have thanked them nicely for the compliment while silently thinking they were crazy.

Yet here I sit, writing the final few words of said book, while both of my kids are happily entrenched in their sophomore year of college, living off-campus, not too far from the same dorms where we dropped them off with tearful goodbyes. They are thriving. And so am I.

The last 18 months have been full of learning. For all of us. Has it been an adjustment that was unpleasant at times? You bet. There were days when I thought the tears would never stop and times when I questioned my own sanity, wondering "What is wrong with me? They're only off at school!"

Did I ever believe that I'd make it to this point, comfortable in my own skin, satisfied with my just-right quiet house and not tearing up at the slightest memory of them? To be totally honest, not really. But thanks to the grace of God, the luxury of time and the healing it provides, and great kids who know their mama's heart, I can honestly say that my husband and I have come to embrace – and yes, even enjoy – the empty nest. It is my hope that the same will be true for you.

About the Author

Photo by Dulce Photography

Liz Yokubison is a former marketing professional who worked at Fortune 500 companies and academic institutions before pursuing her love of writing. Her work has been published in national and regional publications such as SKI, Yoga Journal, Skiing, Women's Adventure and Park City magazines. Prior to writing her first book, she was the editor for jans.com and was instrumental in launching their affiliate site, whitepinetouring.com. Liz holds a bachelor's degree in marketing and an MBA from Michigan State University. A proud mother of college-aged twins, she lives in Park City, Utah with her husband, Ron and their rescue dog, Cooper. You can follow Liz on her website, www.lizyokubison.com and on her Facebook page: What Now? Musings of an Empty Nest Mom.

Made in the USA
Las Vegas, NV
18 May 2021

23274778R00106